Breaking Dementia

Breaking Dementia

FINDING ACCEPTANCE AND HOPE FOR THIS JOURNEY

Rick Phelps
with Leeanne Chames

PC Publishing Group

Cover design and interior by www.ebooklaunch.com

ISBN: 978-0-578-43590-9

This book is dedicated to you, the reader.
Our prayer is that throughout these pages you will be encouraged and find strength and hope for this journey.

ALSO BY RICK PHELPS

While I Still Can

A Word from Rick

Since our first book, "While I Still Can...", many requests have come in to write another. I told myself when I finished that book, there would never be another.

Well, never is a long time. Our dear friend, Leeanne Chames, has co-authored this book with me. We knew there had to be a second book and that we were being called upon to write it.

You will get answers on many topics from me, a dementia patient, and from Leeanne, a caregiver.

The title, Breaking Dementia, says it all. It is exactly what we have been trying to do ever since I was diagnosed. Break down the myths and break down the stigma.

Breaking down the questions that come when this horrible diagnosis is thrust upon a family:

What do we do now? How will this affect us financially? How will our loved one be treated? What legal steps should be taken? Should a dementia patient be driving?

This book answers these questions and many more. Just like in the first book, "While I Still Can...", what you read here is fact. Not conjecture, not something that may happen, and not something that I read and am passing on to you the reader.

What you read here is how I as a dementia patient have learned to live with my disease. We confront major questions, we cover topics that no one else is willing to discuss.

This book will give you a look into the world of a dementia patient and the world of a caregiver. It is our hope that it will bring you peace, knowing that you are not alone in this journey.

We can't cure or fix anything, but we can walk this journey together "While we still can"....Breaking Dementia.

I want to thank God for giving me the strength to do what I do. I want to thank Him for everything I have and everything I ever will have.

I want to thank my wife, Phyllis June. She is my rock. She knows me better than I know myself. None of this would have been possible without her courage and love that she gives to me every single moment of the day.

And my family. Not only my immediate family for what they do for me, but my extended family, Memory People. We have over 19,000 members in our online support group family, a number that is growing every day.

I may be the Founder of Memory People, but I have said since day one, if not for the people there, sharing their stories and reaching out and helping each other, none of this would be possible.

What we do on Memory People is so simple, we talk to one another.

We share our deepest thoughts about dementia. We share things with other members that we cannot even talk about with our own families, for one reason or another.

If you are a patient, a family member, a caregiver, or if you have lost your loved one, you are invited to join us. You may be someone that just wants to know more about dementia, you are welcome also.

You can find us on Facebook, just type "Memory People" into your search bar. We would love to have you. Walk with us on this journey, Breaking Dementia...together as it should be.

A Word from Leeanne

They say into every life a little rain must fall. If you or someone you know has been touched by Alzheimer's disease or any type of dementia, it is certain that you've experienced more than a little rain. It could better be described as a torrent of adversity like you've never known.

This is how dementia has affected my family, having lost my Mother to Vascular dementia and my Mother-in-law to Alzheimer's disease. It's turned my world upside down and all our lives will never be the same.

In the face of these and other types of dementia to which there is no cure, and which so utterly and completely devastate us, all can seem hopeless. We are here to tell you that is not true.

This book is about acceptance and hope that empowers us to face each day and helps us to break the grip of dementia on our lives. Not just to survive these days, but to live them to the fullest.

Throughout this book you will learn how to think in new ways, to let go of your fear, and to accept what is happening. You will find accurate, helpful advice and information, and you will know that you are not alone.

Acceptance gets us from this moment to the next. It takes away the struggle in our hearts and minds. It embraces knowledge, brings hope, and builds bridges to each other. Bridges of love, compassion and relationship from patient to caregiver and caregiver to patient.

Drop your guard for a while. Open the eyes of your heart and take this journey with us.

My unending love and deep gratitude to my husband, Louis, for always encouraging me, counseling me, and supporting my passion to help people who are caught in the grip of dementia.

My deep thanks to our beautiful and amazing kids who have shown such support and patience in sharing their Mom with those in need. And special thanks to our daughter, Mary, for all her help in the editing of this book. I can never put into words how much you each mean to me.

Lastly, but always at the top of the list, is my Father in Heaven who makes all things possible. He is my life, my breath, and hope for all my tomorrows.

May you find insight into the world of dementia, and peace for your journey, as you walk this with us.

CONTENTS

Introduction

This book was written by a patient and a caregiver, it is a compilation of writings which span the last 8 years. Throughout the chapters you will see realism and authenticity as the struggles and trials of this journey of dementia unfold. It has been lightly edited to provide an easy, clear reading experience while preserving the spirit of the authors' thoughts.

We have never referred to ourselves as professionals. We have no degrees in dementia or certificates of completion for dementia courses taken.

What we do have is experience as a patient and as a caregiver and a passion to help and educate people from the wealth of knowledge that comes from living this personally.

Rick, as a person with Early Onset Alzheimer's disease, and Leeanne, as someone who helped provide care to her Mother who had Vascular dementia and to her Mother-in-law who had Alzheimer's disease.

When you are looking for information about a disease and how it affects a person and those caring for them, there is no better place to go than to those who are dealing with it in real life. Experience is truly the best teacher.

Our goal throughout this book is to support and educate. If you find information that is helpful to you, then we have accomplished that goal.

If you have questions about medical procedures or diagnoses or if you need medical advice or professional support, please consult your doctor or the appropriate professional resources.

We have provided a Resource section at the conclusion of our book, there is much helpful information there.

As we say in Memory People™, we take what might be helpful and we leave what doesn't apply. And we are thankful for it all.

We hope you are blessed as you take this journey with us. We are Breaking Dementia, together.

CHAPTER 1

DIAGNOSIS: DEMENTIA.
NOW WHAT?

By Rick Phelps

So, you have just been diagnosed with dementia; Alzheimer's disease, Lewy Body dementia, Vascular dementia, Early Onset Alzheimer's, or another type. Or, your doctor may not have specified what type of dementia may be causing your symptoms.

In any case, the questions are the same. Now what? What do you do? Where do you go for answers? Whom should you seek out for help?

These questions come up often in Memory People, our online support group on Facebook. The reason for this is because too often, a patient does not get the information they need when they receive a diagnosis of dementia.

When you are diagnosed with dementia, you need to understand what it means, what the future will bring, what you need to do next, and what you should plan for.

In my book, "While I Still Can...", the very first chapter is titled "Seventeen Minutes".

It took exactly seventeen minutes from the time my wife, Phyllis June, and I arrived at the Neurologist's office until the time we left with my diagnosis of Mild Cognitive Impairment/Early Onset Alzheimer's disease.

We were like so many others. We weren't told anything. The neurologist said, "you have signs of Early Onset Alzheimer's. I am writing you a prescription for Exelon Patches and I will see you in six months".

That was it. We had no idea what to do. We drove home in almost complete silence because we both knew that if we even began to talk about what had just happened, we would likely lose it.

All of this could have been avoided. All too often, the neurologists, doctors, or whomever you are seeing, don't tell you the things you need to know when they give you a diagnosis like this.

This is my advice for what to do after receiving a diagnosis, from a patients' perspective, one that has been living with Alzheimer's disease for ten years or better.

The day you get this diagnosis you are not any worse when you leave the doctor's office than you were when you walked in.

For some reason, family members and patients sometimes believe that once they have an official diagnosis, they will suddenly start a drastic decline.

This is simply not true. Take some time and don't do anything for about a week. Give this time to set in.

Then you can start making your plans. This is very important because most of the time, the first plan you make simply won't work for the duration of the disease and all that is going to happen. If you don't know this by now, you will learn it.

After the initial shock wears off, you will need to get some affairs in order. These affairs are different for every individual and situation. We started with getting our financial affairs in order. We went to our attorney and put everything we own in Phyllis June's name.

We put our house, our vehicles and our camper in Phyllis June's name. I don't have anything in my name. We did this for a couple of reasons, and your attorney or financial advisor will work with you on what you need to do for your situation.

Next, we made Phyllis June my sole power of attorney over my medical directives and our finances. Again, this is something your attorney can explain to you.

Then, I went on a personal crusade to learn as much as I could about dementia. My neurologist should have given me information about my disease, but it was up to me to learn about my diagnosis and what my future now held.

When doing your research, the number one thing to remember is that you cannot believe everything you read on the internet.

Whatever is posted on any given site is no better than the person who posted it, which is why we monitor our posts so carefully in MP.

You won't see posts about things that are simply not true, or about something that someone heard from some source, somewhere. We deal in facts and reality, not concoctions, conjectures, or false hope.

You can find pages on Facebook that will tell you what you want to hear about dementia. They don't tell you what you need to know about it, and that is a very important difference.

Take, for example, what is called the "Virtual Dementia Tour". This was created by someone who does not have dementia of any kind. How can someone who does not have dementia create a program like this and then tell you that it is, indeed, what dementia patients experience? They can't. But it is being done all the time.

Some "experts" in the field of dementia have been using this VDT for years. I can tell you that this program is nothing like having dementia.

I don't walk around like I have marbles in my shoes. I don't have the sensation of having headphones on my head, blaring noise in my ears and rendering me unable to understand directions. The reason I can't understand directions is because I have a brain disease.

When I or other patients talk about "foggy" days, it has nothing to do with our eyesight, as this Virtual Dementia Tour would have you believe.

And I don't fumble around with my hands like I have oven mitts on. This entire program is a misrepresentation of dementia but there are people who swear by it. No patients that I know of agree with it, but those who claim to be the "experts" certainly do.

This is all about money. There are billions of dollars made every year off these diseases by people who create programs and concoctions to "help" you. Don't be one of those who wastes your money on these things.

Remember, you are not going to suddenly take a turn for the worse simply because you were diagnosed yesterday. It is just a diagnosis.

Will your disease progress? Yes. Is there anything that has the capability of slowing down the progression? No. Is this diagnosis terminal? Yes, but the reality is, we are all terminal. We are all going to die.

Some types of dementia progress slower than other types. Some patients progress much faster than other patients. No one knows why. Only time will tell how your journey will be.

I would put myself in the mid-stage of this disease. And this is another thing that I would encourage you not to do. Do not pay too much attention to the "Seven Stages of Alzheimer's".

Your loved one can be in "stage two" this morning, and then be in "stage four" by this afternoon. They could be in what is termed as "stage three" for months, and they could stay in "stage five" for years. There is simply no rhyme nor reason to these diseases and how they affect a person.

There are three stages that you should be familiar with. The early stage, the mid-stage, and the late stage.

We are all in an early stage when we first notice signs of memory issues. This slowly, but surely, progresses.

Then you get to the mid-stage, where everything can be an issue. Every patient is different as to what they will struggle with in the mid-stage, and to what degree.

I can still drive. I don't drive very much, maybe three times a week, and I never drive very far. But there are other patients in the mid-stage who cannot drive at all. As I said, every patient is different.

The late stage can last weeks, months, or even years. There is increased confusion, inability to do the simplest of tasks. Mobility issues are more pronounced and eating and feeding oneself becomes a struggle.

Again, symptoms and severity are different for every patient. Educate yourself using reputable resources so you have an idea of what is coming.

After you have educated yourself on dementia, what you need to do is focus on today. Not what might happen six weeks from now, six months from now, or even six years from now. Don't worry about what is coming.

Your loved one may be diagnosed with dementia and not doing all that bad, and then they're in a car accident and they are gone. We never know how long we have here on this earth, so we shouldn't dwell on the future.

Don't compare patients to each other, don't compare another patient to your loved one. We are all different, just like every human being is different. Our finger-prints are unique and so is how our brains work. And, how dementia affects each of us is different.

Get through today, then get ready to do it all over again tomorrow. Today might very well be the best day your loved one has, ever.

We get hung up on the little things. "Dad is refusing to bathe". "Mom won't eat today, or she refuses to eat". "My husband argues about everything". "My wife seems to sleep too much".

Though each of these things seems terrible at the time, they really are nothing compared to what is coming. Take one day at time.

Another thing to keep in mind, is, do not think that your loved one needs to be entertained or busy all the time. They don't. Not all of us want to do word puzzles or brain teasers. Some of my best times are spent just sitting here, doing nothing but relaxing.

Remember, people with dementia are dealing with memory loss, confusion, anxiety, personality changes, and much more. Everything that happens, everything we do, and everything we don't do, always comes right back to that.

It's the disease. It's always the disease.

Chapter 2

The Purpose of Mini Mental Tests

By Rick Phelps

One of the first things you will be advised to do if you are having difficulty with your memory, is to go to your doctor and get a Mini-Mental Test.

Which is not bad advice at all. You just need to understand what a mini-mental test is and what the results mean.

I have often said that you will know when you have dementia. When you experience bouts of memory loss that occur more often than normal, you notice it.

And, I know it's hard to believe, but trust me, this is like no other thing you have ever experienced.

When we think of dementia of any kind, especially the most common, Alzheimer's disease, we think of memory loss. And, obviously, there is memory loss with dementia of any type.

But there is much more to it, which we cover in the following chapters of this book.

Regarding mini-mental tests, they are very simple. It is a noninvasive set of tests that can be done in a matter of minutes in your family doctor's office.

They consist of several tasks one must do. For example, you will be asked to draw a picture of a clock with the hands at a certain time. You will be asked to name several items in the room, and then the doctor will come back in a few minutes and ask you to repeat those items from memory.

You will be asked to name several animals. You will be asked what day it is, what month it is, and what year it is. They will ask you who the president of the United States is.

You will read a short story and then in a few minutes you will be asked to repeat certain parts of that story. These a few examples of a mini-mental test.

The reason for doing these tests is to help the doctor get a grasp on what your cognitive ability is. The thing to know is, this is just a test. It is not a definitive way of diagnosing Alzheimer's disease, or any other type of dementia.

A mini-mental test is not a "pass/fail" test. Its' purpose is to give the doctor some insight into your cognitive ability. They will note that you are probably nervous, apprehensive, and under a great deal of stress and they have a scale that adds all of this into the equation.

As I said, a mini-mental test should never be given to determine if a person has dementia. It is simply a tool. A tool that is used to gain insight into what may or may not be going on.

Sometimes you will hear someone say, "Mom did horrible on her mini-mental test, she has Alzheimer's". Sometimes this is said out of fear of the unknown, and sometimes it is said because of the ignorance of dementia. Alzheimer's disease cannot be diagnosed solely from the results of mini-mental testing.

This does not make someone an ignorant person, it simply points to ignorance about these diseases and the purpose of this testing. This kind of misinformation is common.

Depending on the outcome of the mini-mental testing, you may be asked to do additional testing. This is the beginning of a search, a search for answers as to what is causing the memory loss and cognitive issues.

These additional tests could include, but are not limited to, thyroid testing, a CAT scan, and blood work. They will also check for any kind of blockage in your arteries. All of these, and many more tests, may be done.

Then, when these tests come back, depending on the results, the doctor will determine the next course of action. It may be prescribing medication for thyroid issues, or the memory issues may be found to be stress related. The reason for the memory loss and cognitive decline may have many different causes.

It is then that your doctor will decide if you should see a neurologist. I have seen three different neurologists and all of them have diagnosed me with Early Onset Alzheimer's disease.

Getting a diagnosis is a long, drawn out process. It may begin with a mini-mental test, but they are not, and should not, be used to diagnose dementia. It took me two years from the time I noticed I was having issues with my memory to the time I received my diagnosis.

My doctor wanted to blame my memory loss on the stress of my job and the loss of my daughter. I was having terrible stress, but it was brought on because of my inability to remember, not because of my job or anything else.

It is also very important, prior to your doctor's appointment, that you have some sort of long-term health care insurance in place.

Doing this could save you hundreds of thousands of dollars. You will be able to get long-term health insurance after getting a diagnosis of dementia, but you will pay dearly for it.

Mini-mental tests are a useful tool, but not when used exclusively for determining a diagnosis. If your doctor has determined that you have Alzheimer's disease, solely based on the results of your mini-mental testing, you need to get a second opinion.

CHAPTER 3

IF YOU'VE SEEN ONE DEMENTIA PATIENT, YOU'VE SEEN ONE DEMENTIA PATIENT

By Leeanne Chames

If you and I were both diagnosed with brain cancer today, would we be in the same place in our diseases at this time next year? Would we have the same symptoms and be reacting similarly to treatments that our doctors might have tried?

If we were both diagnosed with diabetes, heart disease, or any other disease or illness, would it be affecting us in the same manner, 5 years from now?

This is important to think about, this issue of comparing people who have diseases and illnesses. It's important because it happens often with people who have dementia.

Interestingly enough, you don't tend to see this kind of comparison with people who have other diseases, but it is very prevalent in dementia. People who have dementia are compared to other patients and questioned why they are still able do some things and not, other things.

There is a saying about dementia. "If you've seen one dementia patient, you've seen one dementia patient".

This means that no two people with dementia are going to be the same. Their progression, their abilities, and the way that their dementia affects them, is going to be different than how it affects someone else.

This is the way it is in all diseases and conditions. No two diabetes patients are the same, and no two cancer patients are the same. Their symptoms, how fast their disease progresses, and how it affects them, is always different. Even two people with the common cold will have differing symptoms and duration of their illness.

This is important to understand, because we can fall into a trap when we compare patients. When a person with dementia is not progressing the same as someone else, or they have different abilities at their stage of the disease than someone else has, we start to wonder why. We may even begin to question their diagnosis.

This is the beginning of stigma. Thinking that a person should be a certain way or have certain abilities to do, or not do, certain things, because they have dementia.

This kind of thinking can also create legitimate worries if you are a caregiver and your husband is bedridden, nonverbal and on pureed food. You may see or know of another patient who was diagnosed around the same time as your husband, but this other patient is still able to converse, enjoy a hobby or two, and even go out to dinner on occasion.

You may begin to ask yourself, 'what am I doing wrong?', 'what have I possibly missed?', and, 'why is this other patient doing so much better than my loved one?'.

Comparing other patients to your loved one can bring an enormous amount of worries, frustration, depression, and guilt.

They say that each person is as individual as each flake of snow. Even identical twins have their own personhood, their own soul, and their own footprint in this world.

That does not change once you are diagnosed with dementia.

Please take this to heart, it is so important.

It is a brutal thing to be given a terminal diagnosis and then be questioned if it's true because you are "doing so well" or you're "not as bad as my loved one".

There isn't anything that one can do to speed up or slow down the progression of Alzheimer's or other types of dementia.

There isn't anything a caregiver can do to buy their loved one more time or control how their disease is affecting them.

As hard as it is, we need to let these things go and accept what dementia has brought into our lives, and, how it has brought it.

I know it's hard. It's hard because we have no control over what is happening, and we are desperately trying to make sense out of this.

I wish something did make sense in this. I hope and pray that more will, in the years to come.

For right now, we need to accept what this is and what it is doing to each of us individually, and to all of us collectively.

This act of acceptance will end the stigmatizing of people who have dementia. It will be a blessing to every patient who will hopefully never be questioned again about the abilities they have, or the validity of their diagnosis.

And it will be a blessing to caregivers, who think they must have missed something because someone else's loved one is doing better than their loved one is.

This is the truth. Take these things to heart, and let that stuff go.

CHAPTER 4

THE FOGGY DAYS OF DEMENTIA

By Rick Phelps

Foggy days. That is how you will hear many dementia patients describe what they go through at times. As a patient, I know exactly what this means.

Some caregivers and family members think this means that their loved one cannot see clearly, like things look hazy, as in a fog. This for me, as a patient, is not the case.

Foggy days means that the person with dementia simply cannot think clearly. Everything in their mind is confused, or "foggy".

Some patients do have issues with their eye sight, but to me, the term foggy days is about confusion and difficulty dealing with people or things that are around. It is trying to know what is going on and trying to decipher what is being said when there are two or more people talking at once. It is not about having a hard time seeing things, as in a fog.

Every patient is different, and some may experience some issues with their eye sight. When you hear the term "foggy days", know that they, the patient, are most likely referencing the fact that they cannot function well. They are mentally confused, not comfortable with where they are or with what is going on around them.

People listen to what the "experts" have to say about what dementia patients experience, when these experts, in fact, have no first-hand experience and therefore no real idea what they are speaking about.

I only need to mention the Virtual Dementia Tour to make my point. This is the exercise where they place headphones, gloves and goggles on a person, and then place marbles in their shoes to mimic what it's like to have dementia. This exercise does not have any similarity with the symptoms of dementia, and I speak more about this, later in the book.

This is what I tell everyone. If you want to know what it is like to have dementia, you'd have to ask a patient. Alzheimer's is the only disease, that I am aware of, in which so many people who don't have it, somehow know what it is like to have it.

You don't see anyone explaining what it is like to have leukemia or diabetes or heart disease. But you can find thousands of people who describe what it is like to have Alzheimer's disease or other types of dementia, and these people don't have Alzheimer's disease or any type of dementia.

This really gets under my skin. I have dementia, Early Onset Alzheimer's, to be exact. One of the fastest progressing types of dementia, so the studies say.

I have officially had this disease since 2010. I had memory issues for at least five years prior to my official diagnosis, so I have been living with dementia for over 10 years. I can explain to anyone what it is like to live with this disease. I know what I am talking about.

The problem is, hardly anyone asks. I think this stems from people not wanting to pry or to get too personal with a dementia patient. You will find that many patients do not want to discuss what they are going through, and that is fine.

If you want to learn about foggy days and dementia and how it all affects a person, ask someone who has dementia, not someone who calls themselves an "expert" in the field of dementia.

CHAPTER 5

FAMILY THAT IS ABUSIVE, HURTFUL, AND DOESN'T HELP

By Rick Phelps

We all have them, family members who are never around and yet seem to know everything. The ones that you cannot please, no matter how hard you try.

This kind of family member never considers helping when it comes to the issues of caregiving, yet they are always ready to give the caregiver their advice on what to do and how to deal with their loved one.

What to do with family that is like this? I can tell you what my wife and I did, and this does not mean that anyone should follow suit; it's just how we dealt with this issue.

When I was diagnosed, an important piece of advice that was given to us, was to try to stay away from stress of any kind. I would have to retire from my career. I would have to make changes in my life, starting immediately.

Those who offered this advice were right. Most people put up with a lot of hurtful and unhelpful things from family members. That, for me, was about to change.

My wife and I simply began to ignore those who thought they knew everything about our situation. They may have had the best of intentions, but they did not know or understand what either one of us was going through.

What I am trying to get at is, when you have dementia, you simply will not be able to deal with hurtful family members who cause stress for you or your caregiver. It is O.K. to admit this, and to give yourself permission to not allow this stress in your life.

A caregiver and a patient are under an enormous amount of stress just dealing with dementia day after day.

A brother or a sister, a parent or a cousin or even a good friend can unwittingly cause an enormous amount of stress in your situation. You, as a patient or a caregiver, must know when to draw the line.

Remember, a caregiver's number one concern is for their loved one. If you are a caregiver, God knows, this takes up 120% of your time.

You can try to be rational about your feelings with these kinds of people, and explain to them how their actions and words are affecting you, but the bottom line is, most people will never change.

Over time, dementia changes everything in your life. Sometimes, that may need to include changes in dealing with the people who are in it.

Chapter 6

You Didn't Do This

By Leeanne Chames

If you know someone who has Alzheimer's or another type of dementia, do you think they did something that caused it, or that they can do something now, to stop or reverse it?

There are many opinions regarding diets and lifestyles and other things that are said to be the cause of Alzheimer's and other types of dementia. Articles are published regularly that attempt to point a finger at why we're getting these diseases.

Because of this, I think it is very important that we are careful with what we accept. This can include products that promise to prevent, reverse, or cure dementia, or, information that promises to do the same.

We need to watch out for peddlers, scammers, and those who prey on the vulnerable. There are thousands of them selling their diets and programs and telling you what you need to do and how you can fix this.

They lead us on wild goose chases, knowing that we are desperate for help.

They want you to think that they are wise and insightful and that they have found the key to this, the key that no one else is telling you.

Please take this to heart. Those who do this are not wise and insightful and they have not found the key to this that no one else is telling you.

Never throw caution or common sense to the wind. Always do your homework. Always remember that if something sounds too good to be true, it truly is.

This line of reasoning, that we have this because we did something or that we still have it because we're not doing something, leads to terrible things.

It leads to things like guilt, blame, resentfulness, and despair.

Don't go down that road. Do not allow guilt about why this has happened or why you're still dealing with it, to get a foothold in your mind or in your heart. These feelings never lead to anything productive.

'They' do not know why we are getting these diseases. That is the bottom line, and I think the healthiest thing that we can do is accept that simple truth.

It is always good to strive to be as healthy as possible, to eat right, exercise, and get enough sleep. That lifestyle always puts us in the best place we can be when we face any disease or illness.

But the truth is, none of these things, or any other thing, is the cause or the fix for Alzheimer's disease or other types of dementia.

My husband and I have some very dear friends who found themselves on this road of dementia several years ago, after the wife was diagnosed with Alzheimer's.

Her husband had a terrible time accepting that this was happening and that there was nothing he could do to fix it.

Every time I saw him at our support group, he would hand me a little slip of paper. It would have the name of a product that he had seen on T.V. or read about in a magazine. It was a product that promised to fix your memory.

He would ask if I had heard of it and what I thought about it. He wanted to know if I thought it would help her.

In his despair and heartbreak, all he was able to see was a cure. All he could put his energy into was hoping for something to come along and save his wife.

That thing, the cure or product that could stop this, never did come along and sadly he sunk into a depression that no one could rescue him from.

He was never able to wrap his heart around this, to live and love today and let go of the only hope he had. A hope for a cure.

When hope for a cure is all that you have, it creates disappointment and sadness, time and time again.

Don't allow that to happen. If you are in denial about what is happening, you need to work to push through that.

The best treatment for this is a therapy called 'acceptance'. The best fix for this is accepting that we cannot change it or fix it.

Once we do that, we are able to walk each day together, making the most of what we have, even in all the pain and heartbreak that this journey brings.

This act of acceptance brings a new hope and a new ability to live and love to the fullest, each day.

Worrying, and getting mentally and emotionally sidetracked, asking why this has happened and wondering how we can fix it, does just that... it sidetracks us from the most important thing we have, the gift of each other and the gift of this day. Don't let that happen.

Accept this. Deep down where it counts, accept that this is happening and that you cannot fix it.

That will do more for you than any diet, product or program could ever promise to do.

Chapter 7

Unwilling or Unable?

By Rick Phelps

Are dementia patients unwilling or are they unable? Which is it? In my opinion as an Early Onset Alzheimer's patient, it's both.

Patients are both unwilling and unable to complete some tasks. They may be unwilling and unable to do just about anything at any given time depending on the progression of their disease, how long they have had it, and what part of the brain is being affected.

The reason I say that it's both unwilling and unable, is because these actions stem from the decline of one thing; the brain.

It is hard for many to comprehend this because we cannot see what is wrong with our loved ones. We can't see if they are unable or unwilling to understand what we are saying to them. We cannot see if they are unable or unwilling to shower, to go out, to eat, to drink, to be around people anymore, and on and on.

All of these things happen, because they do, indeed, have a brain disease. A disease that you cannot see ravishing their body, as you would be able to see if they had cancer, for example.

In a terminally ill cancer patient, you are more able to see the decline. If a person has COPD, again, you can see their issues that they have with breathing.

A terminally ill dementia patient looks virtually the same as they always did, for a good portion of their disease. The fact is, we have trouble understanding what we cannot see.

People often say to me, "You look like you're having a good day". What does that mean? How am I supposed to look when I am having a good day, versus, how I look when I am having a horrible day?

I tell people that I no longer have good days. What I have are bad days, horrible days, and sometimes, incomprehensible days.

We lose sight of this because our caregivers and the people we see every day cannot see what is wrong with us.

A person who breaks a leg is unwilling to walk simply because they are unable to. I am unwilling to comprehend what is being said in a conversation of two or more people, simply because I am unable to comprehend it.

All of this is happening, not because I am stubborn or because I just don't care, but because I have a brain disease.

It really is that simple.

CHAPTER 8

THERE IS NO MAGIC PILL, BUT THERE IS MEDICATION THAT CAN HELP

By Rick Phelps

When your loved one becomes aggressive, either verbally or physically, what do you do?

It is always important to first rule out pain or infection that may be causing their change in behavior. If infection and other causes have been ruled out, then you can explore medications that can help these behaviors.

You never know when a patient may become aggressive and abusive, how long it might last, and how bad it might get.

Medicating your loved one does not mean that they will be in a zombie-like state. That is never the goal. The goal is to lessen the aggression.

Medications can help combat aggression, anxiety, depression and more. It can take weeks to get the right medication at the right dose that will help your loved one, or you may be fortunate and the first drug that is prescribed will work for them.

You do not want them to be medicated to the point that they can't function. I am on many different medications; for anxiety, depression, and stress, etc. I would not be able to function daily without these medications.

I don't feel drugged, but the people that are around me can tell that I am on them. My wife can see a difference in me and I do also, when I forget to take them.

The goal with using medications is to find that happy medium where you can function as a human being. The proper medication at the proper dosage will help keep the dementia patients' emotions in check.

Even with my medications, though, I still have bad days. Every patient does, and we always will. The important thing to remember, is, if your loved one has anger issues, you must deal with them, because they will get worse.

Verbal abuse almost always leads to physical abuse. Do not let this happen. You and your loved one need to get through some very rough times. If it becomes world war three every time you suggest to your loved one that they take a bath, you need to see their doctor and get them some help.

Patients need to be medicated for these behaviors, it is very important. You cannot wish this away or just hope that the aggression or abuse will stop. Neither the patients nor the caregivers are safe in these situations.

There is no magic pill, but there is medication that can help.

Chapter 9

Caregiving: An Investment of the Heart

By Leeanne Chames

Caregiving is an investment, not only of time and energy, but of our heart. You can be long distance from your loved one, seldom see or touch them, and still be their caregiver.

Your loved one may live in a facility where they are receiving most of their care, but you can still be their caregiver.

There is no perfect caregiver. There is no caregiver that doesn't have the same questions and feel the same emotions that every other caregiver does.

Am I meeting their needs? Should I be doing something different, something more, something less, something for me, something for them? These are common questions that caregivers ask themselves.

I believe that if we could really see each other's dementia journeys, we would realize how level of a playing field we are all on.

That is what dementia does; it is the great equalizer. No one, with any amount of money or fame, can change their journey or the outcome of it.

There are no 'privileged caregivers' that have access to the best, most expensive drugs that can stop this or slow it down. There are no 'super caregivers' who have this all figured out and don't struggle and agonize over it, like all other caregivers do.

Dementia takes those who have little and those who have much, and it brings us all together on the same playing field.

It takes those who are highly educated and those who didn't finish high school, and it says, here is your fellow man. And we see each other and realize that you are me, and I am you, and there isn't anything that either one of us can do to fix this.

We are all in this heartbreaking journey, together. Caregiving is an investment of the heart, whether we have a little or a lot, whether we provide care at home or in a facility, and whether we live close by or far away. Bless us all in this journey.

CHAPTER 10

THE DEAD END OF ARGUING

By Rick Phelps

Early on, dementia patients begin to lose the ability to argue, but that doesn't stop them from doing it. Many times, my wife and I will get into a small disagreement about something, usually something that doesn't matter.

I would say that 98% of the time I am right, in my own mind. The reality is, it's more like 10%.

What happens is, I try to explain my side of things, the way I see things and what makes perfect sense to me.

My wife has learned to just agree to disagree. Unless, of course, it is something that affects our finances, our safety, or other things that are too important to just let go and count as 'small stuff'.

If a dementia patient tells you during an argument that they are 100% correct, it is because in their mind, they are.

I try my best not to argue with anyone about anything. Long ago I lost the ability to make decisions and do the simplest of things, so arguing is something that my wife and I just do not do.

She does allow me to win what few disagreements we do have, and I know this. I sometimes think that I really have convinced her that I'm right, when the reality is, she is agreeing with me because it is just simpler to do.

I can't speak for all dementia patients, but this one tries his best not to argue. I just can't take the stress, and in the end, it's not worth it.

Never argue with a dementia patient. The chances of you winning are slim to none. That, of course, doesn't stop the dementia patient from arguing with you. Just know how to deal with it, is the only real answer.

CHAPTER 11

IT'S THE DISEASE,
IT'S ALWAYS THE DISEASE

By Rick Phelps

It's the disease, it's always the disease. I have said this for years now. I know some people get tired of hearing it. I get tired of saying it. But it is, indeed, the truth.

If your loved one wanders off, it's usually not anyone's fault. They can be walking from the kitchen to the front room and then, for whatever reason, they walk out the front door and end up blocks or even miles away.

Can you stop this? Not always. There are things that you can do to help ensure that wandering is kept to a minimum. They can carry some sort of GPS device on them. You can install an alarm pad on their bed and an alarm of some sort on every door in the house. I tell caregivers to take a minute every morning and take a picture of their loved one.

This way, if they do wander, at least you have a recent photo to show the police when they ask for one. You know what your loved one looks like, they don't.

Everyone has a cell phone and it takes but a second to do this. It can save a life.

Wandering is just one of the issues that caregivers face. Choking has always been a fear of mine. I am not likely to choke to death any time soon but in my years of EMS I have seen the outcome of people choking, and it is many times, not good.

A person with dementia can eventually lose the ability to know how to swallow. Not all do, but some. They lose the ability to do everything at some point, because of the disease.

Take, for instance, a mother who has dementia. She is in her 80's. Preparing a meal for twenty people is not a problem, in fact, this is what she has done her entire adult life.

Now, she takes it upon herself to cook. The implications of this can be disastrous. Fire is the number one thing that comes to mind, especially if she is cooking at three o'clock in the morning and everyone else is sound asleep.

Bathroom mishaps are not the patient's fault, nor are they the fault of the caregiver. These can occur daily, and the number one reason for it is the disease.

What I am trying to say is, things happen. And everything that does happen is not without reason. It is the disease that makes the patient do what they do.

No one intentionally leaves a pan on the hot stove and just walks away. But I have done this, many times.

No one would intentionally become aggressive with their grandchildren or any family member, but this does happen. It is the disease that makes a patient become verbally or even physically abusive.

I wish there was an answer. Even a complex one would do. The best answer I can come up with, is that the disease makes the person with dementia do the things they do.

It's always the disease.

CHAPTER 12

I'LL BE YOUR MEMORY

By Leeanne Chames

Why can't your loved one remember what you just told them? Why can't they remember that they already had something to eat, or that you come to see them every day?

Why can they not remember these things, but they can remember things that happened 30 years ago? They may clearly remember the day they got married, or the day they met their spouse. They remember their children being little, and family trips and places that they've been.

I've heard it explained that it's because of the way that dementia affects the brain; where the disease starts and how it progresses, at first taking short-term memories and then, eventually, long-term memories.

And then, sometimes, they can remember things that just happened, or they can't remember something from long ago. They remember something today when they couldn't remember it yesterday, or vice-versa. There is just no rhyme or reason.

This is such a wild ride for everyone. I see patients get frustrated because they can't remember. Caregivers try to keep up with all of this, never knowing what the day will bring. Joy, or heartache. Connection, or confusion.

Truly, one disease, many victims.

There is but one thing that helps us deal with all of this, and that is to accept it. Writing notes for our loved one, explaining things to them, reminding them... convincing, debating, arguing... none of that works.

Acceptance always works. We must accept what is happening and how things are. We still won't understand, and we still won't like it. It will still break our heart into a million pieces.

Acceptance doesn't make everything better, but it does enable us to live in the reality of our loved one's world.

Our loved one is living in the reality of their dementia. Every patient is, because they have no choice. Some deny it, but they cannot stop what is happening to them or how the disease is affecting them.

The people who aren't living in the reality of this are those around them. Those that do not accept this and make necessary changes. We, as caregivers and family members, need to make changes in our thinking to help us adjust to what is happening and to help us let go of how things 'should be'.

Denial is believing that someone with dementia 'should be' able to remember.

Denial puts up walls of 'why can't you remember', and 'come on, I just told you that'. Acceptance tears down those walls and instead builds bridges of love, compassion, and relationship.

When our loved one tells us that they never get out, and we know that the reality is that we take them out every day, acceptance says, 'oh no, that's not good. We'll go for a walk today'.

When our loved one cannot remember what day it is after we've reminded them for the 10th time, acceptance says, 'it's Tuesday', and it gently answers the question, again.

Acceptance is not easy and it doesn't fix everything. What it does do, though, is it allows the caregiver to step over into the world of dementia, the world where their loved one lives.

And then, we are truly walking this together.

CHAPTER 13

IT'S O.K. TO ADMIT THAT IT'S NOT O.K.

By Rick Phelps

I cannot begin to cover the many ups and downs of this caregiving journey. When your loved one does something that is unthinkable, don't think for a moment that this is the worst that things are going to get.

The one common denominator in all of this is that there is no common denominator. There is no figuring this thing out, there is only dealing with it.

Everyone, at one time or another, throws their hands in the air and says, "I cannot do this anymore". Even if they never admit it, at some point they say it. And it's alright to say that. As a matter of fact, I implore caregivers to say this. There is nothing wrong with saying, "I just can't do this anymore".

When you say this, you have not given up. You have not lost. You have simply come to the realization that you have done all that you possibly can to care for your loved one.

Does this make you a quitter? Does this mean that you do not care for your loved one as you once did? Does this mean that you have simply given up? No, not in the least.

What it means, is, you have faced reality. And, it means that you may be saving your loved one's life. In my career in law enforcement and in over 24 years working in EMS, I have seen many cases where the patient should not have been cared for at home.

Sometimes it is because the family doesn't want to place their loved one. Or, it may be because they are in denial. And, sometimes, it is because they want the money that is being brought into the home by way of their government assistance.

There is no down side to placing your loved one too soon. There are all kinds of downsides in waiting too long to place them, and none of these downsides are good.

I cannot thank caregivers enough. As a dementia patient, I realize what it takes to be a caregiver for a dementia patient and I have set into place the most important thing I can for my wife and our family.

Long ago, I stated in my will that I want to be placed when the time is right. It is up to Phyllis June, and not anyone else, to know when that time is here. She doesn't have to ask anyone's permission, she will know when the time comes.

This is a burden that I lifted for her because I can, and because it was the right thing to do.

Caregivers need to know when it is time to ask for help. You need to have a plan and then have another. And you need to know that it is perfectly fine to say, "I cannot do this anymore."

I cannot thank the caregivers of the world enough. I have been in your corner since the beginning.

I have lobbied for caregiver funding in Washington D.C., I have told your story, through my story. Thank you, all of you.

CHAPTER 14

THE REAL DEMENTIA TOUR

By Rick Phelps

I attended a dementia symposium several years ago and their keynote speaker was very good, until she picked two people from the audience and invited them to join her on stage. They proceeded to do a demonstration of something called the "Virtual Dementia Tour".

The audience members were instructed to take off their shoes and they were given shoes that had several tiny balls inside. They were given glasses that looked to be smeared with Vaseline.

On their heads they placed headphones that were playing loud noises, and they were given heavy rubber gloves to put on their hands. The lights were then turned down low and the audience members were told to look for three items that had been shown to them before the exercise began.

What I remember is how the audience laughed as the two people stumbled around on the stage, bumping into things, running into each other, and never finding one item, let alone the three they were supposed to find.

They were each given a round of applause and then sent back to their seats. Then the speaker said, "This is what it is like to be an Alzheimer's patient."

My wife had to hold me to my seat. I couldn't believe it. I guess this "experiment" goes on in many training sessions. This tells me why so many health care workers know so little about dementia patients, let alone their disease.

They laughed. It haunts me still. I had just witnessed the most degrading thing I had seen about Alzheimer's disease.

If you ever have the opportunity to see this demonstration, please say something. It does not portray what an Alzheimer's patient experiences.

In EMS I used to make life and death decisions in a matter of minutes. Sometimes, seconds. Now, I open my sock drawer and I just stare at it, unable to make a choice, and almost all my socks are white.

I delivered three babies. Now, I check the mail that's delivered, even if I have already gotten it out of the mailbox. Over and over during the day, I forget, and I go out and check the mail, again and again.

On two different occasions I performed CPR and advanced life support on an infant. One lived, and one didn't. Now I wonder if I took my medication. Where is it, and what if I have forgotten to take it?

I once was involved in saving the life of a teenager who had been in a horrific automobile crash. He never should have lived, much less been able to walk again. Now, I sometimes can't figure out how to unlock the doors on my jeep, let alone remember where the button is to put the window down.

I worked a case locally with many other law enforcement agencies that led to the capture and arrest of a serial killer. He had taken the lives of five people, all of whom he shot with a high-powered rifle at long range.

I recently bought two BB guns for the kids at our camper. I can't ever remember where the BB's are supposed to go.

You see, when you have this disease, everything changes. It's not only memory loss that you deal with, it's the loss of your very identity. You lose who you were, and what you once did.

I don't want to get all dramatic here, but the worst thing to lose is your mind. The only thing worse than that, is knowing that it is happening.

I'm going to go look for some balls to put in my shoes and some rubber gloves to put on my hands. Then I'm going to walk around with blinders on. Trust me, all of that would be easier than living with this disease, day in and day out.

CHAPTER 15

THERE IS NOTHING EASY IN THIS JOURNEY

By Leeanne Chames

Alzheimer's disease, or whatever type of dementia that we are dealing with, can bring us to places that we never could have imagined.

Places of frustration, anger, depression and anxiety like we've never known. These words, 'there is nothing easy in this journey', started running through my mind so long ago, as we encountered heartbreak after heartbreak with my Mother-in-law's diagnosis of Alzheimer's.

I know this is so much easier said than done, but as caregivers we need to try and get all the breaks and rest time that we can. Take advantage of services and day programs if you're able to. Any time that you can take care of yourself, find your center, and do things that you love to do, will be a benefit to both you and your loved one.

Never feel ashamed for seeking out some type of counseling, whether it's from a local church (many pastors provide counseling), or from your local Family Services. Check with them for counseling resources.

We all get to the end of our rope with this every day, and many times a day. We need a place to let that steam off, to let go of the frustration and anger that has built up, so that we don't let it off on our loved one.

We know that they can't do a thing about what is happening to them. We also know that they can't do anything about how this is affecting us. Even when they are angry, mean or belligerent, and even if we think they are being this way on purpose, the fact is, they still can't do a thing about it.

The patient cannot change or stop what the dementia is doing to them. They can't let things just roll off their backs or stop themselves from saying what is on their minds. And even if there is a momentary understanding that something hurtful was said or done, it will be a fleeting thing.

This isn't because they don't care, it's because, increasingly over time, dementia doesn't permit a person to think beforehand, respond, and then remember to correct themselves so that it doesn't happen again the next time. That is just not how dementia works.

Dementia diseases are progressive. They will get worse, and the amount of care and patience that is required for full-time caregiving is going to have to increase to meet those needs.

Realizing that these needs have surpassed what a caregiver can provide is so important. Just as important, is realizing that this is no fault of the caregiver. It is solely the fault of dementia.

Think about what you will do in the future for you and your loved one, and have a plan for it. Our goal as caregivers is to have as much peace and calm as possible, for everyone involved.

That is always the best place to be.

CHAPTER 16

YOUR LOVED ONE IS CHANGING. THE QUESTION IS, ARE YOU?

By Rick Phelps

"You must come into my world", is something that I have often said, as a patient. This is because I can no longer go into yours.

Caregivers can sometimes get overly concerned about what works or what doesn't work, what to do or what not to do. What I encourage caregivers to keep in mind, is, what works today, may not work tomorrow. And, it may not work ever again.

So, what do you do? This is when coming into our world becomes so important. No one can know what is happening or understand what we are going through. I am a dementia patient and even I don't know what is happening, most of the time.

Caregivers must to learn to adapt and change with the changes. I hate to compare dementia patients to children, but this is a very good analogy.

You may have prepared scrambled eggs for your one-year-old, for breakfast. They love their scrambled eggs. Then, one morning, they don't. They spit them out and will not eat them.

Trying to figure out why they suddenly won't eat the eggs that you fixed for them, is futile. What you do is, you don't feed them scrambled eggs tomorrow, and maybe not for a long time.

In many ways, this is the same with a dementia patient. If your loved one refuses to get dressed, it's not in anyone's best interest to try to make them do it. It's also futile to try and figure out why they are refusing to get dressed.

If they decide that they don't like the television on, you better not have it on. If they decide they're not going to the doctor, all the coaxing in the world is not going to change their mind and get them to go.

In other words, in each of these scenarios, there is one constant theme. Don't try to force a dementia patient do something. Now, if it has to do with their safety or the safety of others, of course, you must intervene.

Explaining to a dementia patient why they cannot do something is futile because they will not be able to understand. In the heat of a situation, it can be easy to forget this.

It is normal to get a shower or a bath every day, but, for a dementia patient, it can be devastating. The feel of the water from the shower and the fact that the doors are closed can be extremely difficult. The vulnerability of getting undressed, in the first place, can be overwhelming.

The main thing, is, you must change your thinking and accept that it's O.K. if your loved one doesn't bathe every day. This, of course, does not mean that you don't see to it that their hygiene is taken care of.

Sponge bathing with a soft wash cloth, using dry shampoo, and finishing with some body powder can suffice for the in-between times.

The point I am trying to make, is, I cannot keep some of the crazy things from happening. No dementia patient can. At times, caregivers can begin to feel that their loved one is able to do something, but they won't do it, because they are trying to upset their caregiver.

I can tell you, for me, this is never the case.

Then, there is the issue of hoarding things. Patients do not have the capability of doing this. In order to hoard something, you must first have a plan. One must take whatever it is that they are hoarding, plan to put it in a certain place, and then plan to get it later. All the while, remembering their plans.

This simply does not happen in the world of dementia. People call it hoarding, because that is how it is easily explained. What the patient is doing is simply putting things where they think they belong.

I can't tell you how often I have put things where they don't belong. Does that mean I am hoarding them? Not at all. It means if you find the bread in the oven, that is where I thought it went, when I was putting it away.

If my wife finds things where they don't belong, she simply puts them where they should be. Many times, she doesn't even mention anything to me about it.

I can't begin to tell you the number of things that I have thrown away. From silverware, to glasses, to toothpaste, to unopened jars of peanut butter. Why? No one knows. I don't realize that I am doing this. It's not normal to throw away the beaters after mashing the potatoes, but I have done it many times, and I will do it, again.

Regardless of what the 'experts' say, you will not be able to figure out why patients do the things that they do.

Why do some patients have such a difficult time when it begins to get dark outside? Some 'experts' will tell you to turn on all the lights in the house. They believe that the patient is having difficulty because the sun is going down. Turning on the lights, therefore, addresses the problem, and will 'fix' it.

This increase in difficulty later in the day has been termed "sundowners". I can tell you, as someone who suffers from sundowners, if we turn all the lights on at sundown, I will still be confused, nervous, anxious, and scared. I will just be all those things, in a well-lit home.

Sundowners has nothing to do with sunlight or the lack thereof. I can have issues of sundowners in the middle of the day. I can also have it first thing in the morning.

This is how my disease affects me. Your loved one may be just the opposite. We are all different, and what works for one, might not be helpful for someone else. Or, what works today, may not tomorrow, or ever again.

Think about this. As bad as your loved one is today, it may be the best day that they will ever have again. We simply don't know. There are good days and there are bad days.

Most of my days are bad, with a little bit of good throughout each day. I know what is in store for me today, tomorrow, and the next day. I just don't know if I will ever have a good day, ever again.

Nothing can change this, but you can help, by coming into our world. We simply can no longer function in the world you live in. The one we used to.

It's not there anymore. And it never will be.

CHAPTER 17

WHILE WE STILL CAN

By Rick Phelps

We built a shed. Many of you are thinking, so? But this feat was huge for me, as are many things that Phyllis June and I do together.

You see, when you have this disease, you slowly but surely lose the ability to do the things that you once could. Things have been this way for me for a long time now.

I cannot do the simplest of things without direction from someone. It is very important that the caregiver helps the patient do the tasks that they no longer can do themselves.

We could have called our son-in-law and he would have had our shed together in no time, but I wanted to do it and Phyllis June knew it would be good for me.

She took control, but she also allowed me to think that I was doing what needed to be done. She read the directions and walked me through them slowly, step by step.

When I made a mistake, she said, "What do you think if you tried this?", giving me the feeling that I was accomplishing something.

As a caregiver, it's not always good to just do things for your loved one. If they are in the early to mid-stages, they need that sense of accomplishing something.

I could never have done this on my own and I would not have attempted it without her. Working together, "team work", as Phyllis June put it, we finished it.

The directions said it could be put together in minutes. It took us three hours and I had no idea it had taken that long, time means nothing to me now.

The important thing here is that I, as a patient, was given the opportunity to accomplish something. Not alone, but it still made me feel that I can be useful.

When you are always doing everything, even things that your loved one can do, you are indeed taking away their dignity. Every person needs to feel that they are contributing and helpful.

Help your loved one do things. Let them know that you are there to help if they need it, and encourage them in projects that they want to accomplish.

I know I could not have done this on my own, but, with the help of my wife, I did get it completed. And most importantly, she did it in a way that she was never condescending.

It's the little things that mean the world to a patient. And our new shed was just what the doctor ordered.

CHAPTER 18

TO: ME, FROM: DEMENTIA

By Leeanne Chames

Ever since I lost my Mom to Vascular dementia and my Mother-in-law to Alzheimer's disease, I have often walked back in time, kind of down 'memory lane'.

I've thought about things that happened that were so heartbreaking and crazy, I still cannot believe it all.

If you were to tell someone who hasn't gone through this, what kinds of things can happen in this journey, they wouldn't believe you. I sure wouldn't have.

I found myself in a world that you can only understand if you've lived in it. And even at that, you don't really understand it, you just learn to live in it. Like trying to learn a foreign language and live in a foreign land.

It will never be your natural language, and everyone will always be driving on the wrong side of the road. You can get good at speaking the language and learning where to drive, but it will never be normal or natural for you. That is what it's like, living in the world of dementia.

As I've thought back on this journey, I have discovered gifts that dementia gave me along the way. Yes, I said gifts.

I can't tell you how hard it is for me to admit that or to feel thankful for any bit of these diseases that took away the people that I love.

As hard as it is to admit this, I also can't fully express how grateful I am for it.

My Mother-in-law was always a very independent woman, to put it mildly. She loved much and did much for others. She would always rather do for you than you do for her.

Alzheimer's gave me a way to do for her. And it wasn't just doing things, it was being with her, calming her, and holding her hand. She became so vulnerable and we had so many precious times of connection and love, that I know we never would have had, had this disease not come along. Gifts.

Alzheimer's also gave me the gift of appreciating today. I had never realized how much I wasn't living in this moment, until dementia came along and forced me to live right now, in this moment, today.

At some point, I realized that the past was really gone and was not going to come back, so spending time wishing things were like they used to be, was a waste of time.

The same goes for living in the future. It wasn't here yet. I realized I shouldn't borrow trouble.

What is going to happen? How will I get through this? I had to train myself and consciously work on not living in the future, not letting the worry of what might happen and what I knew was going to happen, take away from today. That still is one of my biggest challenges in life.

I want to say something about this gift. This gift is like the candy that you suck on and is very sour at first. You can hardly stand having it in your mouth. But you're persistent and you don't spit it out and after a bit, you realize you've made your way down to the sweet part.

Letting go of the past, and not letting your heart and its worries and fears wander into the future, is like that candy. You get past the bitter, to the sweet.

You focus on today, and then you're able to appreciate and treasure the sweetness of right now. It's not easy. You go through all the tantrums, and feeling like it's not fair, but you will never regret doing this. You'll never regret living in today. It is a gift.

Another gift. It made me realize that no matter who you are, things can change just like that and your whole world is upside down. No one is immune or safe from dementia. So, do like that saying goes, "love much, live well, laugh often." Do that as much as you possibly can. You won't ever regret that, either.

With my Mom and her Vascular dementia, there were gifts, too.

She was delusional from the very beginning, and I became a calming voice for her. She would call me in a terrified panic and I would calm her down, or try my best to. It was so strange how the tables turned, me, now becoming a calming voice, for her.

To have that happen, to provide a voice of reassurance and comfort for her, when she had done that for me all of my life... how can I express the honor of that and the gift in that.

The biggest gift in this journey with my Mom and Mother-in-law was that it did not take away what we were, or what we had together.

That doesn't make a lot of sense, but I had never lost people in my life like this before. I thought I was going to lose it all when I lost them, but I didn't. Their dementia took them from me, but it couldn't take what we had, our memories, and our love. I still carry those things in my heart for both of us, and I always will. Gifts.

I have much to be thankful for. As utterly devastating as dementia has been in my life, and continues to be, it has given me gifts, and I will be forever thankful for them.

CHAPTER 19

LOSING TIME, ALL THE TIME

By Rick Phelps

Lost time. Dementia patients experience this. I would like to have the time back that I have spent over the last few years, just looking for things that were right in front of me.

I have had an issue with recognizing things for a few years now. What I am looking for can be right in front of me, but for whatever reason, I do not recognize the object and keep looking for it, until I finally just give up.

Lost time can also affect a caregiver. I would bet, on any given day, most caregivers lose two hours a day just looking for their loved one.

This doesn't mean that their loved one has wandered out of the house. It's the time spent going from room to room looking for, or checking on, their loved one.

We know there isn't any way to fix this, it's just one of those things that you rarely hear about. Lost time.

Here is another facet of lost time with dementia. I can be sitting in my recliner, just thinking about things, or staring out the window, for what I think is just a few minutes. But the reality is, it could have been an hour or more that I have been doing this.

Long ago, I lost the perception of time. I can still look at a clock and see what time it is, but I have no perception of what that time means. This, too, is a form of lost time for dementia patients.

Some may feel that there are much more important things to worry about than the time your loved one may be losing. But this is a very important part of life that dementia takes from a patient. It is a struggle, especially for those who are still cognitive enough to know that they are, indeed, losing time.

What to do about it? There is nothing that can be done, just like with other symptoms of dementia. You cannot fix this.

I lose time, and time is my enemy. I don't know if I have six years, six months, six weeks, or six days to be able to communicate and do the things that I can do, now.

Many times, when a patient is stressed, worried, agitated, or even becomes physically abusive, one of the reasons could be as simple as, they have lost time. They don't understand what is happening, and they react the only way they know how.

Lost time. Just one more thing we will never get back.

CHAPTER 20

IT'S A MATTER OF TRUST

By Rick Phelps

Trust is something that most people take for granted and simply don't think much about. As a person who has Alzheimer's disease, I have no choice but to trust everyone around me.

Most people think it starts and ends with your spouse or caregiver. Someone close to you, that you as a patient have put complete trust in.

The truth is, it goes much further than that. From the time that I open my eyes in the morning, I must trust people. It begins with Phyllis June, of course.

But all throughout the day, no matter who I talk to or who I encounter, I trust that they will do what they say they will do. That they will not take advantage of me, if you will.

I have no concept of being taken advantage of, anymore. I know right from wrong, of course. I may go to the local market and get a gallon of milk. I can give the cashier a twenty-dollar bill and if they give me back $2.95 I would simply thank them and be on my way.

Don't ever think that there are not people out there that you will come into contact with, that will not take advantage of you.

I go through my day saying "yes" a lot. No matter what the question is, 99.9% of the time, I must believe people and agree with them, trusting that they will not take advantage of me.

I have no concept of time. I trust that the people who are around me will remind me when I need to be at a certain place, at a certain time. No longer can I trust myself to know or remember these things.

I mix up information often. I trust someone else to make sure that what I am saying is the truth.

I don't do any interviews without either Phyllis June or Leeanne with me. I cannot trust that what I say will be what I want to say.

I never want to lead people astray or fabricate anything. I trust in the people around me to make sure that what I am saying is accurate.

It is difficult, at best. Keep in mind, dementia is so much more than just memory loss. It affects everything the patient does.

Patients are told to stay away from stress. What people don't understand is that simply not being able to function the way we once could, is stressful, itself. You cannot get away from the disease in your head.

I had to write this out before I posted it online. I do that every time. I cannot trust that what I want to say will be accurate, so I write my thoughts down and then I go over what I've written, again and again.

Then, after typing it out online, I try to read through it once more, which I can never do. I can only trust that people will understand what I am trying to explain.

Trust. It's what patients depend on. It never hurts to tell your loved one "Trust me, I will do the right thing for you, always."

CHAPTER 21

EVERYONE DESERVES RESPECT

By Leeanne Chames

When does a person with Alzheimer's disease, or any type of dementia, become unworthy of respect?

Is it when they start wearing adult undergarments, 'diapers', because they have become incontinent?

Is it when they can no longer feed themselves because their brain no longer remembers what to do with a fork or a spoon?

Maybe it's when we think they are too unaware to realize that we are talking about them. Or, possibly, it's when we think they can't understand, anyways.

I have a friend whose heart hurts to this day for how her mother was treated by the staff at her nursing home. My friends' mother loved to dance, and the staff enjoyed getting her to dance, for their own amusement.

"Come on Betsy (I've changed the name), let's see you dance!"

She would get up and start dancing, and they would stand there and laugh. "Look at her go!"

They treated her like an object for their own amusement. It was an exercise in control, complete disrespect, and abuse.

Of course, sometimes a person with dementia will hear music and get up and dance, as anyone might. However, creating a situation like this for one's own amusement is wrong.

Betsy's daughters' heart would break when she saw this. My heart breaks too, when she talks about it.

As caregivers, friends, and people who care, we owe it to any person who has dementia to be looking out for their best interests. We need to be aware of people like this, people who abuse those who are vulnerable.

If you see disrespect, say something about it. Be the voice for the person who has lost theirs.

If you see abuse, do something about it. Even in fun, even when everyone thinks that it's cute, if it's at the expense of a person with dementia, it is wrong.

Speak for those who cannot speak for themselves, for those who are taken advantage of and disrespected. Everyone deserves respect.

CHAPTER 22

SAM THE SERVICE DOG

By Rick Phelps

If you are thinking about getting a service dog for your loved one, I would encourage you to do your research.

One of the most important things to remember when seeking out a reputable service dog trainer, is to try to find one in your local area. It is imperative for the patient/owner to have the ability to be involved in the training.

All of my involvement in my service dog's training was through phone calls, emails, and text messaging. Everything worked out for the best, Sam is an excellent service dog.

An important thing to know, is that many people who have dementia do not want to draw attention to themselves and having a service dog does draw attention. Wherever I go, I am constantly barraged with questions about Sam and with people wanting to pet him.

Even though Sam wears a vest that plainly states "Working Service Dog, Do Not Pet", people constantly ask to pet him.

In the beginning of Sam's training I was concerned that this was going to be a problem, and it has been. It's not my fault, and it certainly is not Sam's fault.

This is a perfect example of people who do not understand Alzheimer's disease.

Service dogs are not for everyone. The patient needs to have the ability to control the dog and give basic commands. As with owning any other animal, there is a sense of responsibility that comes along with owning a service dog.

In my opinion, the patient must be in the early- to mid-stages of dementia when considering a service dog for them. Service dogs are highly intelligent animals.

I am constantly asked what Sam does for me, as if he can "fix" any of what I am going through. He can't.

He gives me freedom and a sense of security, as I am never out of his eyesight. On a scale of 1 to 10, Sam has taken my stress level that was about a 12, down to about a 3.

The only issue I have is the attention that he brings to me.

If you are considering a service dog for your loved one, make sure that you find a reputable trainer that is as close to you, as possible.

Sam helps me in ways that no medication has. He cannot "fix" anything, but he does help to alleviate some of my symptoms.

Chapter 23

I Have Alzheimer's, I am Not Stupid

By Rick Phelps

Two of the most difficult things that I deal with as a patient are stigma and the lack of understanding about dementia.

When I do a speaking engagement, people tell me that they are amazed that I can share about what I go through and how this disease affects me and my family. Most people are of the mindset that every dementia patient should be exactly the way their loved one is.

My wife and I will be the first to admit that before my diagnosis, we had little knowledge of dementia. Phyllis June did not know that Alzheimer's is a slow progressing disease with no cure, and that it is, indeed, fatal.

Since my diagnosis, we have taken time to learn all that we can about it, and one of the things we have learned, firsthand, is that there is a great deal of stigma and misinformation about this disease.

In their minds, most people picture an Alzheimer's patient sitting in a wheel chair and staring out a window. This is what their loved one does, so this is what they perceive every patient does.

They are surprised and even taken aback by the fact that I have thoughts and opinions, and that I can express them. They are equally as surprised to hear that I drive and do other things that their loved one can't do, and maybe could never have done.

When I share my story, it never changes. Years ago, I asked my case worker, "why can I articulate when I speak of my disease or share about it online?".

She explained that this is because I am passionate about it. She said, "Things that we are passionate about, stay with us longer".

I have been diagnosed with dementia, Early Onset Alzheimer's, to be exact. Even though I have this, it does not mean that I can no longer know or remember anything.

I have lost many things to this disease, as many patients have, but I am still at the point that, at times, you might not realize that there is anything wrong with me. Chances are, in the beginning of their dementia, your loved one was the same.

Be educated and informed and don't compare patients. Be thankful for what your loved one can still do.

CHAPTER 24

WE ARE MORE THAN OUR MEMORIES

By Leeanne Chames

I recently heard a doctor say that Alzheimer's is a disease that steals the soul.

It didn't take me even one moment to know how wrong of a statement that is. It is also the reason why we can never judge whether someone's life has worth anymore.

When we see that a person can no longer walk or talk, if they can't recognize their loved ones or remember anything, we can begin to feel that their life is not worth living.

But we must realize that we are more than our memories. We are more than what others can see of our abilities.

We are loving, feeling, eternal beings, and nothing can take that away. The fact that there is still breath in us is proof that our life is still worth living, no matter what.

No matter if we have cancer, or we are blind. No matter if we have Multiple Sclerosis, Parkinson's, or Diabetes. And, no matter if we have dementia.

Breath is life, and while we still have breath, we have worth and value and all the reason in the world to live.

We must hold on to this in this journey, especially as dementia takes more and more all the time.

Even if we cannot understand or it doesn't appear that our life is worth living, we are still here, and life is still worthwhile.

Despite all that it does take, dementia is not able to take our spirit or our soul.

Bless us all in this journey.

Chapter 25

I Am Losing Myself

By Rick Phelps

Phyllis June and I had a long talk last night, and I told her that things were not alright.

I have been getting worse, which is no surprise, but the sensation of it is getting the best of me. She wanted to know how I know that I am getting worse. What is going on? What is different?

I told her that, among other things, my confusion is getting more frequent, the stress is more intense, and the fear of things is also worse.

One of the things with dementia is, people have questions, and they always want answers.

This is a disease of the brain. Even my doctors don't really know what is happening, or why.

We talked for a while about this, but I don't remember what the conclusion was. I know I brought this up with her so she isn't left out in the dark.

When I used to have bad days, at times, several in row, I sometimes wouldn't say anything. I would just ride them out. Now, that has changed. I can no longer keep it to myself because they are more frequent and worse than they used to be.

The days have turned into weeks, and weeks into months. I have long ago lost track of the perception of time. This thing is like a giant merry go round, on which you can't stop.

The hardest thing about this disease is not only losing your memory but also losing everything around you. And all the while, realizing it is happening.

I have always been the type of person to get to the bottom of things. I would always figure out what was wrong, what the problem was, and then I would find a solution for it. I have only figured out one thing about this disease, and that is that there is no solution.

There is no "fix" for this. I find myself thinking, if things would just stay as they are, I could figure out a way to deal with what is going on. But things change constantly.

I have been told that people who have been diagnosed with Early Onset Alzheimer's disease decline much more rapidly than people diagnosed with other types of dementia. I have no idea if this is true, and for the past few years I have disputed this claim.

But I think now, this may be right. The decline I have experienced in just the past few weeks is very evident to me. Perhaps it is time to have my medications checked, possibly increase some of them. Who knows?

Sleepless nights and nightmares are getting the best of me. I wander around our house like I am in a strange place, when in fact, I am in my own home.

I think every patient goes through this, some just can't explain it.

I am losing my identity. I can't remember from one moment to the next what I am doing, or what I was going to do. I don't comment on the posts in Memory People very often anymore. I am always worried that I will not understand what is going on and will say something that might be detrimental. I would never intentionally do this, but I know it could happen.

Remember, when you see a change in your loved one, chances are that they see it, too. At least, I do. My heart breaks for the caregivers. The ones who must watch their loved ones slip away a little at a time.

Take time to be with your loved one. The most important thing that my wife and I learned in the very beginning of this, was that things must change. You must do what is important to you.

Your lifestyle must change, everything you do must change. Don't spend your time worrying about what is coming. Live for today, right now.

We are doing that, and Phyllis will always have that to be thankful for.

CHAPTER 26

YOU CANNOT FIX THIS

By Rick Phelps

"I can't believe what my husband did." "You are not going to believe what Mom is doing to aggravate me." "Dad knows what he's doing, he's just trying to get attention." These things are commonly said by family members and caregivers.

They cannot believe the things that their loved ones are doing or saying. The patient may be repeating themselves constantly or they might be shadowing their caregiver. They could be constantly flipping the channels on the T.V. or refusing to turn down the volume.

When these things happen, family members and caregivers try to correct or stop what the patient is doing.

Here is something that you won't hear anywhere else, yet it is true. You cannot stop these annoying things that your loved one does. You can try, but it won't work.

As human beings, we are wired to ask someone who is doing something that is annoying, to stop. The problem is, that doesn't work with dementia. If it was that easy, caregivers and patients wouldn't have these issues.

Your loved one may follow you from room to room and want to be by your side every waking moment of the day. This is called "shadowing".

The person with dementia does this because they have a fear of being alone. How do I know this? Because I have done this on many occasions. Once this starts, the only thing that can change it, is the patient.

Some will give you suggestions on how to stop shadowing. In short, good luck with that. What the patient is doing, they are doing unknowingly, and involuntarily.

Your loved one doesn't set out in the morning with a plan to follow you around all day. It is something that they do for a reason, and they cannot help it.

The very best advice I can offer caregivers when these things begin to happen, is to deal with it. I know this sounds simple, and it isn't, of course. Trying to change these things that the patient is doing is just not going to happen.

These quirks will only stop if the patient them-selves, for whatever reason, stops doing them. Your loved one won't follow you around until the day they die. This in time, will stop, if for no other reason than they are no longer capable of walking.

There will also come a time that they won't repeat themselves anymore. They will lose their communica-tion skills, and simply become mute.

About five times every morning, I ask Phyllis June what day it is. She answers me, and then five or ten minutes later, I ask again. Not only can I not remember what day it is, but I can't even remember that I've already asked her, over and over.

Instead of her explaining that she just told me, or trying to help me remember, she simply tells me what day it is. She knows I am going to ask her again in a few minutes.

You see, she has learned that it does absolutely no good to try and figure out how to get me to remember what day it is. I don't have the ability to remember, because I have no short-term memory anymore.

Do this with your loved one. Instead of wasting your time trying to figure out how to help them remember, just give them an answer to their question.

We try to micro-manage and figure out ways to fix what is happening. The fact is, you can't help patients remember. You can't fix this.

It is much simpler, and will help to keep your stress level down, if you just accept that.

Another thing to keep in mind is, as bad as some of these habits are, there are probably worse ones coming.

Don't be surprised about what your loved one is doing. You can try to help them to stop, but it will most likely be a waste of time and you will just become more frustrated than you were before.

CHAPTER 27

A MATTER OF THE HEART

By Leeanne Chames

Dementia is a head condition, not a heart condition.

When your loved one looks blank, it does not mean they have no feelings, or thoughts.

When your loved one does not smile, it does not mean they have no joy.

When your loved one cannot remember your name, it does not mean they do not love you.

While the mind forgets, the heart remembers.

A moment of love and connection produces joy in the soul that is not soon forgotten.

More than a memory, we are loving, thinking, feeling human beings.

Even behind the veil of dementia.

Chapter 28

Where Are You Going? The Deal with Shadowing

By Rick Phelps

When a person with dementia follows their caregiver and always tries to keep them in sight, it is called shadowing. They follow them like a small child would follow his or her parent.

Shadowing can have the Alzheimer's caregiver feeling smothered and like their personal space is being violated.

When I shadow Phyllis June, it's because I have a fear of being left alone; in a store for example, or even here at the house.

One of the first things I lost as a patient is the sense of time. Just a few seconds can seem like an hour, so being alone for just minutes can cause panic because it feels like much longer than that. Thus, you get shadowing.

Now, there are many other reasons why a patient would shadow their caregiver or family member. And there are many reasons for shadowing that you nor anyone else will ever figure out.

The worse the dementia gets, the more likely you will see shadowing. In time it will cease. The patient simply won't have the ability to shadow anyone.

I can only imagine how frustrating shadowing can be to a spouse or a caregiver. Only a patient can explain to you why they have the need for doing this. And many times, they don't even know.

That is dementia. And that is what we as patients deal with every minute, of every hour, of every day.

CHAPTER 29

I AM NOT SUFFERING,
I AM STRUGGLING

By Rick Phelps

I am not suffering, I am struggling...struggling to hold on to what I have and can still do.

With this disease you have a constant worry about what you will lose next. A couple of years ago I woke up and had lost the concept of time. Before that, I had lost the ability to understand any more than two paragraphs of writing.

Suffering is not what I call it. It is struggling. Struggling to hold on to what I have.

All patients are struggling in one way or another. Some can talk about it and some can't.

The best way that I have found to describe what it is like to have dementia, is by describing the effects of a drug called Versed.

Versed is a short-term memory-erasing drug. It is used in surgery, and EMS also uses it quite often. It erases all short-term memory.

Imagine sitting in a room and one by one, complete strangers come in and talk to you as if they have known you all your life. They show you pictures you have never seen, yet you are in them.

Some may even speak in a different language, as if you can understand what they are saying. All of this will indeed cause you to panic. It would anyone.

Sometimes, this is what dementia is like. A person with dementia can be in a room with their family, yet they don't recognize anyone. People can be speaking their language, yet they can't understand what is being said. They are on the verge of panic.

Everything that was normal and familiar, isn't anymore.

Sometimes, a patient will say that they want to go home, when they are home.

What they may be referring to is their earliest memory of home. It could be a childhood home that you might have no idea of, or it could be a home that they have made up in their mind.

For the patient, it is very real. Anytime your loved one begins to say or do things that are absurd, remember that these things make sense to them.

There is a reason for everything the patient does, they simply cannot communicate it.

For me, I am not suffering, I am struggling. There is a difference. The struggles are so profound that inside I am, indeed, suffering. Not from a physical pain, but a mental pain.

Patients are almost always mentally drained from dealing with dementia. When they want to nap in the middle of the day, let them. This can be difficult for the caregiver, thinking that they will be up all night if they sleep during the day. Depriving them of napping is not the answer.

I must have a nap just about every day now. It's not because I am physically tired or even that sleepy. It's because I am mentally drained, and I am struggling.

Chapter 30

Acceptance; the Path to the New Normal

By Leeanne Chames

Deep down, what we all really want is to go back. We want to find our way back to when things were normal, the way they were before dementia came along.

The problem is, this journey changes you to your core. I couldn't begin to be the person I was, even if I was able to find her again.

My Mom is gone now and so is my Mother-in-law, both lost to the long goodbye of dementia. They slipped away after I said silent goodbyes to them for years.

You know those goodbyes. The ones you say time and time again as dementia takes your loved one's abilities and who they are, bit by bit.

You say goodbye to each piece of them lost. You grieve and mourn and then you accept this new normal, and you move on. You do this over and over in this journey.

When I got to the end, I realized, like a final, spiteful slap from dementia, that it had even taken our last goodbye. There would be no final goodbye for us, only for me.

Those who are walking this day by day have only one good choice. Step into this day. Do this day. Whatever that looks like, whatever is happening, it is your new normal and you must accept it.

None of this is easy, but we must stop fighting this and turning away from reality. We must embrace the loss, grief and heartbreak of this journey. When we do that, we will find new paths. Paths to healing and hope.

Acceptance doesn't mean that everything will be O.K. now. It just means that you see and accept what is happening.

It's the best place we can be, with our eyes open, our hearts soft, and living in the reality of this day and this moment. As much as it hurts and as much pain as it brings, there is nothing better than this.

We can't fix what is happening, but we can accept it. We can know that we're not alone and that others care and understand. That really does mean the world.

All of this gives us strength for today, and hope for tomorrow.

We will never be the same, and we can never go back. But there is a path to a new normal, through acceptance.

CHAPTER 31

MAKING PEACE WITH THIS DISEASE

By Rick Phelps

For myself, I try to think about what I have, what I am still able to do, and what makes me happy.

I try to stay away from negativity. People who cause unnecessary drama or try to convince me of the latest cure for my disease. I don't have time for these things.

I prefer to take what time I have left and spend it enjoying the finer things in life.

Like the smell of fresh cut grass. I have cut grass my entire adult life, but until a couple of years ago, I never took the time to enjoy it.

Or sitting in a rain storm, watching one of God's wonders. The smell of fresh rain after a downpour.

These and many more things I try my best to keep focused on. Many patients don't have the ability any longer to enjoy such things. Or they are at a place in their dementia where if they do, no one can tell.

I wonder, did they ever get the chance to enjoy such simple pleasures?

Caregivers struggle to keep things as "normal" as possible from day to day, when the truth is, there is no normal, there is only a new normal every day.

The most useful thing you can do as a patient, family member or caregiver is to make peace with this disease. There is no escaping it and there is no fixing it.

There are those that deny having it or that their loved one is suffering from it. Those are the ones I feel sorry for the most. Dementia diseases progress whether you accept them or deny them.

By accepting this, you are not giving up. You simply understand what is coming and you have made plans for it. You make the best of a horrible situation.

You do this day in and day out until one day, everything you have sacrificed for, everything you love, everything you cherish, is gone in the blink of an eye. And this happens so quick for some, their loved one's progress so fast, that they are left reeling in disbelief.

They cannot believe their husband is gone after having dementia for only three years. The thing is, once you are officially diagnosed, it is said that you have had this disease up to ten years already.

Don't deny this disease. You can hate it all you want. You can loathe it and curse it, but don't deny it. Too many times the years pass by and this disease takes your loved one and then you wake up one day wondering what happened.

That is when guilt takes over. Did you do enough? Could you have done more? Was everything you did for the right reasons?

Here is the bottom line. You can do nothing, or you can do everything. I prefer my wife to do the latter, but this disease will progress no matter what she does.

Don't cry for me when I'm gone, help me celebrate my life while I am here. When this disease takes everything from my mind, I don't want anyone saying,

"If only I would have done this", or "If only we had done that."

The writing is on the wall. I have long ago made peace with this whole process. That doesn't mean I have given up or given in. It just means I will enjoy what time I have left.

I will make the most of the months, years, or however long God sees fit for me to be here. I am heading home, that's where I am going.

The road will be rough, unbearable some days, but I am heading home. I will be in the arms of our Creator for eternity. When HE brings you to it, HE will bring you through it.

CHAPTER 32

FIBLETS, STORIES, AND KEEPING THE PEACE

By Rick Phelps

It does no good to tell a person with dementia about something as painful as a death in the family if they are unable to remember it and deal with the news.

They will have to be told again and again, each time reliving the shock and pain of it. If they are asking to see their loved one who has passed, it is much better to tell them something else, for example, that they are on vacation, or they are out of town. Tell them that they are sick, or that they will be here to visit tomorrow.

Anything is better than telling them something that will devastate them. It serves no purpose. Imagine being told over and over that your brother has died, with the pain and heartbreak of it being new, each time. That is what it would be like.

Lying to a patient seems so cruel, but only to people who don't understand dementia.

I am still at the point that if something horrific happens, I can understand it. Knowing if someone has understanding, is the key. How to know? That is the million-dollar question. They may be able to understand today, and not tomorrow.

I have a distant relative who has dementia. She's in a nursing home. Another family member of mine called last night and was telling Phyllis that she thinks this relative is going "bonkers". She said she's been asking about her mother who's been dead for 40 years.

This family member thought the doctor should give her some "happy pills".

There are no "happy pills" and my relative is not "bonkers". She has dementia. To her, her mother is very much alive. My advice was that the family member needs to agree with her. It does no good to tell her that her mother has been dead for 40 years. This is called using fiblets.

She will never see her mother again, but you don't need to tell her that. You can just tell her, "a visit with your mother would be wonderful".

The doctor isn't going to give her something that will make this better. There is no fix for this.

The best thing to do is to agree with her, it makes everything much easier. In this woman's mind she is younger, perhaps in her twenties or even an adolescent. She wants her mother, she wants to feel safe.

You will hear the most absurd things coming from a patient. People need to understand how to deal with these things. Agree with them, tell them fiblets, redirect them to a different subject. Always remember, to them it is reality, it is their world as they know it.

CHAPTER 33

HELLO, THIS IS DEMENTIA SPEAKING

By Leeanne Chames

Can dementia turn my loved one into someone they never were? Maybe, selfish, or even hurtful?

Yes, dementia can do this. It can turn this person that you have known and loved into someone that you don't know anymore. It is heartbreaking and devastating.

I had a lot of resentment begin to build up in me over things that would happen with my loved one. Something had to change, and for a while I expected that my loved one should change. Eventually, dementia taught me otherwise.

It is so hard when your loved one does or says things that you never could have imagined they would do or say.

What I had to realize was that dementia was a part of them now. It was the filter that all their communications went through, from them to us, and us back to them.

No wonder actions became so confusing, and conversations became so disjointed.

We react to words and actions based on our feelings, our perceptions, and our ability to understand.

When dementia becomes our filter, those feelings, perceptions and abilities are completely thrown off.

People with dementia begin to struggle to understand things, sometimes misinterpreting what people say and do. This can cause suspicion and doubt.

It helped me to remember how my Moms used to be. I had to remind myself that what was happening now was because of the dementia and not because of them.

Honestly, they would roll over in their graves if they had known some of the things that they did and said. And that may be one of the biggest blessings in all of this. I don't think they ever realized or remembered a lot of it, and I am grateful for that.

I adopted a phrase that Rick has always shared, and I made it my mantra. "It's the disease, it's always the disease." These words helped me to not blame my loved one for what was happening. This was very important because I didn't want dementia to drive wedge between us.

Our love and relationship were preserved, and for that I will always be eternally grateful.

CHAPTER 34

DEMENTIA AND WANDERING.
NOT IF, BUT WHEN

By Rick Phelps

"Dad?" This is the one thing you never want to hear yourself saying as you walk through the house in the middle of the night, unable to locate your loved one.

The definition of wandering is: not keeping a rational or sensible course.

To a family who has a loved one with dementia, wandering brings new complications. It is the terror that comes with the realization that your loved one is nowhere to be found.

And terror it is. I describe this as like having your children at an amusement park, and you look around and realize that one of them is missing.

That feeling you get in the pit of your stomach is undeniable. We've all felt this at one time or another. This is what it is like to have your loved one wander off and have no idea where they went.

The first thing you need to do is call 911. Many times, families waste precious time by looking for their loved one themselves. This is fine to do but call 911 first.

If you find them by the time the authorities arrive, that's a good thing. If not, they have more resources at their disposal than you do.

I also tell people that it's a good idea to snap a picture of your loved one with your cell phone every day, first thing in the morning. When they are going to bed is a good idea too.

This gives the authorities an accurate account of what they look like and what they were wearing without you wasting precious time trying to remember or explain it to them.

Too many times I hear that a loved one with dementia has never wandered and that it would be the last thing that would ever happen. Well, it could be the last thing to ever happen. The first time could be the last time, depending on the outcome.

Sometimes a loved one wanders, and they have no idea where they are going, or why. They may have wandered off because they are trying to get somewhere that they feel safe. They may not, for whatever reason, feel safe in their environment.

Trying to determine why people with dementia wander is waste of time. You never will. The only thing you need to realize is that wandering is real, and it can happen to the person who seems content and cared for. It can happen to any patient.

They could be on foot, or if they still drive, they may take the car. When I was in law enforcement, I found an 82-year-old man who had driven his truck through a gate at a prestigious golf course and was driving around in circles when I arrived.

He had been missing for over 6 hours from a community about three hundred miles away. There wasn't a BOLO (be on the lookout) for this gentleman because the family had assumed that he was in their area, not three hundred miles away.

Wandering can happen with any dementia patient, even those whom you would least expect to wander. It can happen over and over, or it may only happen once. Remember, there is no rhyme nor reason to why dementia patients do the things they do.

The only thing to do is to try and prevent this from happening. Bed pad alarms are very useful. They are pads that lay on the bed and when the patient goes to bed they can be turned on. If they leave the bed, an alarm sounds.

I can't tell you the number of times I have heard people say that the only way they could keep their loved one in the house was to install double keyed dead bolts on the front and back doors.

Never, ever do this. There are devices you can get to deter a dementia patient from opening a door, but a double keyed dead bolt is not the way to go.

What if you lose the key? What if there is a fire and you panic trying to get you and your loved one out of the house?

There are devices on the market that can alert you when a door has been opened or your loved one is up and out of bed during the night.

Again, wandering can and does happen. Have a plan and then have another, because chances are, the first plan may go up in smoke.

You simply cannot be too vigilant when it comes to keeping an eye on a dementia patient. There have been thousands of patients who have walked away from facilities that have state of the art alarms. It happens.

Remember, if your loved one wanders, the first thing you need to do is call 911. And when the patient is found, it is imperative that you get to them as quickly as possible. They will be in sheer panic mode.

Sometimes the authorities will bring the patient to you. You need to have your phone handy, so they can call you when your loved one is located.

The authorities will try their best to calm your loved one when they are found. This will likely not work. Even when you arrive on the scene, they might be in such a state of shock that they may not recognize you.

I tell everyone whose loved one has wandered that they need to be seen by a doctor in the emergency room soon after they are located. When being transported, it is essential that you are with them in the squad and never leave their side.

I could go on and on about this topic. I hope that what I have said will enlighten you as to what to expect and what to do, not if your loved one wanders, but when.

CHAPTER 35

ARE THEY SAFE? ARE THEY PAIN-FREE? ARE THEY CONTENT?

By Rick Phelps

As a patient, I want to be safe, pain-free, and content. We all do. Keeping your loved one safe can be done by keeping them within sight, or by placing alarm pads on their bed to alert you if they get up in the middle of the night.

It is important to watch what they put in their mouth. If they are experiencing swallowing issues, you need to watch for gagging or choking. Patients might put anything into their mouths, so be aware of what is accessible to them.

Your loved one may not be able to communicate such things as pain. Can you imagine, for example, having a severe tooth ache and not being able to communicate this to anyone? Or they could have a migraine headache, or some type of infection and be unable to communicate their pain or discomfort.

You may notice that your loved one is blinking more than usual, but you might just attribute this to their disease, when in fact they have an infection in their eye, or their eye ball has been scratched somehow. There is an endless number of things that one must watch for when it comes to keeping your loved one pain-free.

Most caregivers know when their loved one is in pain. They can see it on their face and in their actions. We know that communication can be very difficult for dementia patients, especially for someone in the mid to late stages of their disease. They may not have the ability to express that they are in pain.

Contentment is a state of mind. Many times, I am content when I am just sitting and doing nothing. One of the misconceptions about dementia is that for the patient to be content, they must be doing something.

This can include doing mind games or puzzles, playing bingo or doing crafts. Many times, a facility is chosen because of the group activities that they offer their residents.

As a dementia patient, I can tell you that for me, activities are not an important thing. I don't need to be kept entertained or busy in order to be content.

When you see a person with dementia who used to be busy doing things, and they are now just sitting and staring out the window, we tend to think there must be something wrong.

People don't realize that when you have dementia, there are no breaks. The confusion, memory loss, anxiety, fear, and loneliness are just some of the symptoms that we deal with, constantly. This is extremely mentally draining for patients.

When I am just sitting and doing nothing, I am content. If you tried to have me do a mind game or puzzle, you would be adding to my stress, not helping with it. This is not true for every patient, but it is true for me.

Taking Mom for a ride in the car may have been something she always loved to do. Now, it might be a horrific event. Just coaxing her to get into the car might be too much for her.

Taking Dad to have coffee with his buddies like he used to could very well be way too much for him now. The people, the noise, and being out of his routine might be completely overwhelming now.

Keeping our loved one safe, pain-free, and content is going to be hit and miss, but they are good goals to have.

Chapter 36

I've Never Felt My Heart Break So Slowly

By Leeanne Chames

I have a Facebook memory that pops up every year. It's from Saturday, March 31, 2012. We had invited my in-laws over for breakfast. I was making blueberry pancakes and sausage.

My Mother-in-law had been diagnosed with Alzheimer's disease about three years before that, and we had moved them closer to us so we could help care for them.

She enjoyed being up and around doing things, but you could tell that she was getting increasingly confused all the time.

Still, she seemed pretty with-it that morning. We all sat down and had breakfast together and when we were done, I began to clear the dishes.

I was at the sink when I saw her lean over to my Father-in-law and say very quietly, "why don't you pay her, so we can leave."

There are times when time just stands still.

At that moment, I realized that she didn't know who I was, and she didn't know that she was in our house, having breakfast with her family.

She thought she was in a restaurant and that I was the waitress.

There were more times like this coming. Things got worse, even though I kept telling myself that couldn't possibly happen. Denial.

I've never felt my heart break so slowly.

I wish to God that I never heard the word "dementia", but that was not to be for our family.

Alzheimer's took my Mother-in-law just 6 months later, finally releasing her from its grip.

Of all the things that dementia has taken, including both my beautiful Mom and Mother-in-law, it did give me a few things.

One of them is, it gave me a realization of the importance of today. It made me see that I need to focus on today and stop looking to the future for things to get better or for this or that to happen.

Dementia also taught me to let go of yesterday and how things were. If there is anything in life that teaches you that yesterday is gone and you need to let go of it, I think it would have to be dementia.

I realized that I needed to live and love today, as much as I possibly could.

Depending on where you are at in this journey, there may still be quite a bit to hold on to, or there may be very little. Or, you may be like me and only have memories left to hold.

I want to encourage you to hold on tight. This is hard and heartbreaking and mind-numbing. We get it. You are not alone, we are all in this together.

CHAPTER 37

LIVING IN A STATE OF FEAR

By Rick Phelps

One of the symptoms that I deal with daily is fear, and chances are, your loved one does too.

It's a constant feeling of fear. People ask me, "What are you afraid of"?

My answer is always the same. Everything. I am mostly fearful of the unknown. What will happen? When will it happen? When I have a bad day, how long will it last? Will it ever get better?

When will I no longer know my wife's name? What day will it be that I no longer recognize her?

Will it be tomorrow? Next week? Next month? Will I wake up one day and not know where I am, not recognize any of my surroundings?

I sometimes sit outside a store and then just drive away, fearing what will happen if I go in. Will I forget why I am in there? Will I not know what to say when someone talks to me?

Will my debit card work? Will I remember my PIN number? Do I have any money in the bank?

This is just a mere glimpse of what a patient fears, it hasn't even scratched the surface.

It is a constant feeling that is with me. Some think that their loved one is afraid at night, or they are afraid when it storms, or when someone stops by that they don't recognize.

When, in fact, they could be afraid to just get up from the chair they are sitting in, because once they do, someone will ask them what they are doing, and chances are, by then they won't know.

I cannot fathom going through this without my faith. I was never an extremely religious person. I do believe in God and I consider myself a Christian.

Without my faith, I don't know if any medication would help me. I believe that there is a higher power, and I believe there is a master plan for all of this.

I would be lying if I said that because of my faith, I have no fear. I have fears and anxiety, but it's not because of a lack of faith. It's because this horrible disease is taking a little bit of me, every day.

When your loved one looks as if they have seen a ghost, you may be seeing the fear they have.

Comfort them and tell them you are there, and always will be.

Personally, I don't like to hear someone tell me that everything will be alright. I know they say this to try and comfort me, but I know that things are not alright, and they never will be.

Making peace with this disease is the hardest thing I have ever done, but it was the right thing. Do I wish this never happened? Of course. But I know there is a reason. And I know that one day I will be told, "You did good, my son. You did good".

CHAPTER 38

PLACEMENT. HAVE A PLAN, AND THEN HAVE ANOTHER

By Rick Phelps

Some of the most frequent questions caregivers ask is about the matter of placing a loved one; how will they know when it's time to place, and how does placement work.

This is different for every patient and every situation.

The advice I give them is that there is no down side to placing a loved one too soon, but there are many down sides to waiting too long, and none of them are good.

There are many issues that can arise when caring for your loved one in the mid to late stages of dementia.

In a facility, the medications are regulated and can be changed if need be, usually within an hour. When your loved one is at home and a situation arises, you must get them to the doctor to evaluate them and change their medications. This has the potential to be a disaster and needn't happen if you have placed them.

Another issue is your loved ones' mobility, or lack thereof. Toward the end stages, there is little to no mobility for most patients. A 70-year-old caregiver that weighs about 95 lbs. is going to have a very difficult time trying to get their 180 lb. husband to the bathroom two or three times a night.

This puts them both in danger of falling. The result could be a broken hip, which for some elderly people is a death sentence.

Just trying to bathe the patient, getting them moved from the couch to the bathroom and then from the bedroom back to the couch can be more than an ordeal.

Then, there is the fear that your loved one will leave the house without you knowing. Wandering does happen in a facility, but the chances are much less that your loved one will wander while there. And the response time when someone does wander is greatly increased because of the number of people there to look for them.

Another issue is stress. Anyone who cares for a loved one understands the stress of caregiving. It doesn't matter if you are in your thirties or in your seventies, the stress that this disease puts on a caregiver is the same.

The thing is, if you are in your thirties, you are probably in reasonably good health. If you are in your seventies, you more than likely have several medical conditions of your own to contend with.

Somewhere along the line, you probably promised to take care of your parents, your spouse, your siblings, or whomever. You may have even promised that you would never place them in a facility.

Well, "never" sometimes gets here before we know it. As a patient who knows his destiny and what is coming, I do not want to put my wife or our daughter through these hardships.

I deserve the best care possible, all patients do. Care should never be compromised because of a promise that was made twenty or thirty years ago.

When you have an elderly caregiver trying to care for their elderly spouse, or a daughter trying to care for her Dad who also has a husband and three kids of her own an hour away, it soon becomes a situation that simply won't work.

Nursing homes nowadays are nothing like they were thirty years ago when you made that promise to never place your loved one. Chances are, neither the patient nor the caregiver have been in a facility that cares for dementia patients. Not lately, anyways.

Some assume that when they can no longer do this, they will just take their loved one to a facility and place them. But that is not how placement works.

The only person who can place your loved one is their doctor. This is because of laws and insurance reasons. It is important to understand that you cannot just drive to a facility, get your loved one settled, and that will be that.

Facilities are in business to make money, and there are two ways that they do that. Private pay, or insurance. They don't care how they get paid, but they do want their money, and that is the bottom line.

It is optimal to have some sort of long-term health insurance in place, preferably before the patient was diagnosed way back when.

Because this rarely happens, most have to depend on the money that the patient has, and you may have no idea where or how much that is.

Another hurdle may be whether the facility that you want to place your loved one in, has a room for them.

Sometimes there are waiting lists. Placing your loved one is a process and takes planning.

This chapter could be twice as long and I still would have just grazed the surface on this topic.

There are only two choices that every family member will face in time: you either place your loved one, or you don't.

90% of caregivers will end up placing their loved one for some of the reasons I have mentioned. 10% will have the means and the money to have private care come in to their home.

The chances that you will never place your loved one are slim. You may have promised that you never would place them, but that was long before either of you could have known what you would be facing now.

Do yourself and your loved one a favor and be prepared. Placing a loved one is one of the most loving things you will ever do for them. You are doing something your heart tells you not to do, but you are doing something that your mind knows is the right thing to do.

This is exactly what you said you would do all those years ago. Take care of them. When their needs are more than what can be provided for at home and you seek out placement, you are, indeed, taking care of them.

CHAPTER 39

THE WORDS "CAREGIVER" AND "GUILT" NEVER BELONG IN THE SAME SENTENCE

By Leeanne Chames

You could ask a caregiver that is caring for someone with dementia if they are feeling guilty about anything right now, and they would most likely say yes, they are.

Dealing with feelings of guilt can be a huge struggle for a caregiver, whether the feelings are justified, or not.

We feel guilty that we've done too much or that we're not doing enough. We feel guilty that we can't seem to get our loved one to eat or sleep, to play a game, or to just be content.

Most commonly, caregivers feel guilty over the idea of placing their loved one. Like accepting a bribe of thirty pieces of silver to sell out your best friend, caregivers feel the sting of the worst betrayal ever, over the thought that one day they may have to place their loved one in a facility.

Feeling guilty about this doesn't start after they've placed their loved one, it starts with just the thought of placement, long before the reality of it even begins to appear on the horizon.

Sometimes, no matter how hard a caregiver tries, they can't seem to make their loved one content. This is when the voice of guilt creeps in, telling them that they must be doing something wrong. It's their fault that their loved one isn't content.

Or, their loved one seems to be worse than someone else's loved one, so guilt whispers to them again and tells them that they must be missing something. It's their fault that their loved one isn't doing better.

Then, the inevitable happens in this journey of dementia and their loved one progresses to the point that they need more care than the caregiver can provide at home.

On the heels of that realization are the whispers of guilt, right on cue, telling them that they should have been able to do this. Somehow, some way, they should have been able to singlehandedly provide adequate care and keep their loved one at home, forever.

The twisted lies of guilt go so far as to tell them that if they really loved their loved one, they could have kept them home. Too easily, a caregiver allows these words to take hold in their heart, and they accept these feelings as truth.

Caregiver, do not allow these lies to have a place in your heart.

We must hold them up to reality and examine them. We must ask ourselves if what we are feeling is based on truth.

The reality is, you did not cause this illness to strike your family. You didn't do a thing to make the disease progress. And conversely, you didn't miss something that could have slowed it down. These are all lies that guilt wants you to believe.

What you did do was meet your loved ones needs every moment of every day, to the best of your ability.

And after all of this, after you have provided the best care that you could for your loved one and done all that you could do, progressive dementia diseases will do what they do. Progress.

When that happens, it does not mean that you have failed. All it means is that the disease is following its natural course and now the needs of the patient call for supplemental care. That may mean supplemental care in the home, part time care in a program, or full-time placement.

Seeing our loved one's needs and doing all we can to provide for them is nothing but love and bravery. It is never a cause of guilt.

In this journey of dementia, doing all that we can includes two things. It includes accepting the fact that we cannot fix this, and letting go of the feelings of guilt about that. We are grieving, heartbroken and devastated over what is happening. But we are not guilty for it.

Take these things to heart. If you don't, and you continue to feel guilty for things that you did not cause or have any control over, you will be wasting your time and energy on feelings that will tear you down and sidetrack you from precious time with your loved one.

Let this stuff go. You and your loved one will both be better for it.

CHAPTER 40

RELATIONSHIPS IN NURSING HOMES

By Rick Phelps

Many times, we forget that dementia patients can still have urges that everyone else has, which can include sexual urges.

So, what is to be done about this? Do you as a director of a facility allow this, and if so, how far do you allow this to go?

Some feel that it's fine for patients to have feelings for other patients. The person with dementia has forgotten that they are married and it is very natural to have these feelings.

I don't agree with allowing patients to cohabitate with other patients. Many believe that it doesn't hurt a thing and they are both consenting adults. I say this is not right.

We need to remember what we are dealing with here. The fact that these people must live in a facility due to their cognitive decline, tells you that they have long lost the ability to make rational decisions.

Allowing such behavior creates liability on the facilities part, in my opinion.

Everyone wants their loved ones to be happy and have friends and companions. However, these kinds of relationships have the potential to go much further than friendship.

Urges may still be there, but a patient should not be allowed to act on them just because they want to. In the eyes of the law, the fact that a person has dementia will not be an excuse for rape.

If something as casual as holding hands is allowed, and this takes a turn and leads to other things, the facility will be liable for allowing this to begin with.

If two patients are married to each other, the issue is still, consent. In general, once a dementia patient needs to be placed in a facility, they have reached a point in their disease that they are not capable of giving consent of this nature.

This is something that is rarely discussed, and that is why it needs to be. I was an investigator for the State of Ohio for a six-county area which included many nursing facilities.

I had many cases of sexual abuse, anything from casual contact, to rape. I was astounded with the number of sexual attacks that I had to investigate.

I am not sharing this for anyone to start worrying about something that may never happen. The issue here is to understand that these situations can happen.

This is one of those topics that needs to be discussed, and families made aware of. The urges are there, not in all patients, but all it takes is one.

CHAPTER 41

CAREGIVER DEMENTIA

By Rick Phelps

Caregiver dementia is a term that I use to describe the effects that caregiving can have on a person. To my knowledge it's just a term, but I believe it is very real.

If you know someone who cares for a dementia patient, sit down and have a cup of coffee with them sometime. Talk to them about anything.

Chances are, they will not be the cognitive person that they were before dementia came into their lives. Caring for a dementia patient takes a toll.

It is a grueling schedule and there are no breaks or down times. It also carries a tremendous amount of stress. We all lead stressful lives, but add to that the stress that comes with caring for a dementia patient, and more than likely their caregiver will experience some degree of cognitive decline.

You don't have time to think about anything but your loved ones' needs. You have no idea what is going on in the outside world.

You have no leisure time and no social life. If you were able to get some time to yourself, you wouldn't even know what to do with it, because you are so out of touch with 'you'. All of this can cause a caregiver's cognitive abilities to suffer.

People want to be understanding of what caregivers go through, but until they have walked in their shoes, they can't begin to understand. This is like nothing they've ever done before.

I am sorry for everything that I put my wife through on an hourly, daily, weekly and yearly basis. It never stops, and it is getting worse. I know that Phyllis and our daughter, Tia, will be with me to the end.

I also know that this is taking its toll on them and they feel the effects of caring for me. This is Caregiver Dementia.

To all the caregivers, I say thank you. Even if your loved one can't express their gratitude for all that you do for them, they are thankful. Trust me, they are.

CHAPTER 42

IT'S HARD TO HOLD ON,
IT'S EVEN HARDER TO LET GO

By Leeanne Chames

I truly believe that losing a loved one to dementia is a loss like no other, because of how dementia progresses and its effects on the caregiver and all those around.

In many ways, and to varying degrees, I think caregivers deal with a type of Post-Traumatic Stress Disorder after their loved one passes away.

During this journey they feel grief and heartbreak, but they push those feelings aside over and over. They do this because they are in the middle of providing care for their loved one and they have no time to deal with their feelings. This leads to tremendous emotional trauma by the time they are nearing the end of this journey.

And this trauma doesn't go away. It is added to the final heart wrenching loss, and the caregiver is left with pieces of themselves and shadows of a former life that is so distant now, they cannot see any road back.

So often, I hear caregivers say that they feel like they're not handling this like they should be. They're told that they should be picking themselves up now, dealing with this better, and moving on. After all, it's been a couple of months.

The thing is, when we know that someone has PTSD, we don't say 'hey, you need to deal with it and move on now'. We don't say that because we know that they have been traumatized by a terrifying event.

In my opinion, a caregiver for someone with dementia has been traumatized by many terrifying events, most of them taking place before the loss of their loved one ever happens.

Grief is individual for all of us. Sometimes we're able to find things to help us cope and put one foot in front of the other, and sometimes we aren't. Hopefully the coping mechanisms that we do find are truly helpful and don't add to our problems, like addictions or destructive habits can do.

If we find that we are not able to move through our grief, it's no fault of our own. It is just an indication that we need resources to help take steps in the process of grieving.

I don't believe there is a wrong way to grieve or a time limit on it. Given that, what we don't want to have happen is to get stuck in our grieving. Grief is a process and there are many facets to it, which I don't believe follow any specific order. This is why it looks different for everyone.

Grief that affects us to the point that we can't take care of even the basic necessities of life; eating, bathing, and sleeping, tells us that we need to reach out for help.

Contact your local Family Services or local Hospice agency and talk to them about grief counseling.

See your doctor if you think you might need medical help. This will enable you to put one foot in front of the other and begin to move through the process of grief.

We also have a Memory People support group on Facebook called The Journey Continues. It is a place for our members who have lost loved ones to share about what they're going through and how they're feeling.

None of this is easy and it's not what anyone could have imagined, but we are walking this side of the journey the same way we walked the other side. Together, always.

CHAPTER 43

MEMORY PEOPLE^{TM}, A PLACE FOR SUPPORT

By Leeanne Chames

We've talked quite a bit about Memory People in our book and we want to explain exactly what it is and why it is so helpful for so many.

On Thanksgiving Day, in 2010, after being diagnosed with Mild Cognitive Impairment/Early Onset Alzheimer's Disease at just the age of 57, Rick sat down at his computer, and created Memory People.

He had questions about what he was going through, and he knew he needed support. He knew there had to be others that did, too.

At the time of this writing we are approaching 20,000 members worldwide. Patients, caregivers, family members, health care providers and people who have lost their loved ones. We have people from all walks of life and professions, dealing with all types of diagnoses and conditions.

Rick knew exactly what he envisioned MP to be, and over the next months and years, through hard work, the dedication of our amazing team of Administrators, and the love and compassion of thousands of members, that vision has become a reality.

I found MP a few weeks after Rick had created it. My Mother-in-law had been diagnosed with Alzheimer's disease and I started looking online for information about it, so I could help my husband and his family.

Right away I could see the love in the group, and the heartbreak in the stories.

It was difficult to look down this road and realize that the things that people were going through were more than likely going to happen to us, too. It felt like too much for me, and I left the group after a few days. It didn't take very long before I realized that this was a place I needed to be, and I came back.

I know there is fear in this journey, and fear in reaching out for help and support. Alongside my relief that I had found MP, was an incredible amount of fear.

As a patient and a caregiver, Rick and I understand how other patients and caregivers feel. Many members share how they wrestle with knowing that they need support but find it hard to read what others are going through.

And then there are those who have shared that they never realized how much they needed support, until they found us. And like a cool breeze that starts gently blowing and bringing new peace and resolve, they find the ability to face these days, no matter what was coming.

How can they do that? Because they know they're not alone. They know that there are thousands of others who are listening to them, encouraging them, and standing in this with them.

We often say, 'we don't have a cure, but we do have each other, and that means the world'.

That is the definition of MP. We can't fix this, we have no cure and no way to slow this down. But we do have a very good thing, the best of things, and that is each other. That means everything.

If you are needing support for this journey, join us. You won't find a more loving, supportive group of people, or get more accurate, helpful information, than you will in Memory People.

We don't promise to fix this, because no one can fix it. But we do promise that you won't feel alone, vulnerable, and without resources, as you walk this with us.

We are bringing awareness, changing lives, and walking this journey together, as it should be.

INDEX

Resources

For Dementia Support

For support for this journey of dementia, join us at Memory People, on Facebook. We are here 24/7, 365 days a year. Someone is always here to help you in your time of need. We don't have a cure, but we do have each other, and that means the world.

Contact Memory People

Find us on Facebook, just type "Memory People" in your search bar.

For Legal Advice

An Elder Law Attorney should be one of the first people you call when you get the news of dementia. They can explain what you need to do, how you need to do it, and when it needs to be done. Among other things, they can assist you with end of life directives, and questions about the different types of DNR's and what will meet your needs.

Contact the National Academy of Elder Law Attorneys (703) 942-5711

For Advocacy for the Treatment of Patients

Ombudsmen are volunteers who work on the behalf of the patient. They are who to contact if your loved one is in a facility and problems arise that fail to be addressed and resolved.

Contact the National Ombudsman Resource Center
(202) 332-2275

For Care for People Facing a Life Limiting Illness

Hospice care is a type of care that focuses on pain and symptoms as well as the emotional and spiritual well-being of those who are chronically, terminally or seriously ill.

Contact the National Hospice and Palliative Care Organization
(703) 837-1500

For In-Home Care Resources

The Area Agency on Aging is a resource for in home help, transportation, caregiver respite, etc.

Contact the Area Agency on Aging
(202) 872-0888

For Intervention for Proper Elderly Care

For those concerned that a patient is in a situation where intervention is needed.

Contact National Adult Protective Services
(202) 370-6292

For a Variety of Local Care Resources

Your local Family Services is a good resource for attaining affordable legal information, grief support group information, and in-home services. To find your local Family Services contact information, just search Family Resources and enter your area.

34712436R00094

Made in the USA
Middletown, DE
28 January 2019